YOUR BUSINESS PROBLEMS SOLVED

PAUL JENNER

David & Charles

Newton Abbot   London   North Pomfret (Vt)

To my Father

British Library Cataloguing in Publication Data

Jenner, Paul
   Your business problems solved.
   1. Small business – Great Britain – Management
   I. Title
   658'.022'0941   HD69.S6
  ISBN 0–7153–7646–2

Library of Congress Catalog Card Number 79–51091

Photoset and printed in Great Britain
by Redwood Burn Limited Trowbridge and Esher
for David & Charles (Publishers) Limited
Brunel House Newton Abbot Devon

Published in the United States of America
by David & Charles Inc
North Pomfret Vermont 05053 USA

CONTENTS

INTRODUCTION

In July 1976 Peter Walker MP went so far as to accuse the government of harsh mistreatment of businessmen, causing them illness and even death. In the four years preceding that speech fifty Acts of Parliament affecting businessmen had gone on the Statute Book.

Paul Getty was fond of remarking that to make money 'it helps to be born at the right time'. If you were born just after the last war you were at the right time for the incorrectly despised 'dash for growth', but at the wrong time for most things almost ever since.

Recently, a good deal of lip service has been paid by politicians to the problems of small businessmen. But little has been done – or, I should say, undone. So much legislation has proved detrimental in the long run. Politicians lack practical business experience, and their professional advisers are bureaucrats and professors. Few have even begun to understand, few care to understand, your problems, the problems that all small businessmen have, that keep you awake at night.

I know that you worry about what will happen to you if your business fails. I know that you stand to lose not just every penny that you put into the business, but also, under that personal guarantee you gave when you borrowed money, all your personal possessions including your home. So in Chapter One I describe some of the basics for improving the odds.

I also know that you lack sufficient capital. In Chapter Two I tell you how to make the most of your own resources, what types of loan are available, where from and on what terms and conditions, and how to make your presentation so as to have the best chance of success.

Of course, you will need to prepare figures, and this is dealt with in Chapter Three. You must be able to show profit and loss accounts and balance sheets that give confidence. You will have to draw up cash flow projections and budgets. Before you can do this successfully you must understand what a bank looks for and how it interprets figures. You should know how to produce management accounts for your personal use and how to evaluate projects.

You should also know how to interpret the figures that are presented to you by others. You might be considering buying an existing business – the subject of Chapter Four.

Many problems revolve around the law of contract. It may be that you wish to avoid the terms of a contract by which you had originally agreed to be bound. It may be that the other party has failed to fulfil his part. Chapter Five sets out clearly the grounds on which a contract may be 'broken' and how it may be enforced.

Let me tell you something about your employees. The key ones probably earn more than you do. They keep pressing for a profit share and a say in management. Your sales rep doesn't send in enough orders and you know he gets home at lunchtime on a Friday and takes his holidays in your car. In the factory you've got two or three slow ones who are a bad influence on the rest and they don't lie awake at night because they're protected by a mountain of legislation, and if the business fails the worst that can happen to them is that they lose their jobs. Meanwhile, you have to spend valuable time wrestling with that mountain. Chapter Six aims to make that a little easier.

Finally, what would happen if your company failed? I felt I would like to give not just the law but also an impression of what it is like to go into liquidation. To be forewarned is to allay the anxiety a little. This is Chapter Seven.

Some of the particular problems over which you may be worrying are given at the end of each chapter (with the exception of Chapter Three), and I suggest solutions to them. These often add to as well as illustrate the text and should be read in conjunction with it. To facilitate this the problem numbers, where relevant, are given beside the sub-headings in each chapter.

So the aim of the book is to combine sound practical advice with the essential facts. Often this alone will be enough to help you find a solution to your problems. But every book has limitations. This book cannot automatically update itself to take account of changes in the law between the time of its preparation and the date of your reading it (and in employment legislation in particular changes may continue to be rapid). It is limited by space; I have had to select what I consider most valuable. It is limited by my desire to be readable and, in simplifying, some detail has intentionally been omitted. It can state the law, cite cases and pass opinions on given problems in the hope that you will be able to interpret how the law will apply in the particular circumstances of your case, but it cannot guarantee that. Interpretation is ultimately the function of judges, who not only tell the public what the politicians mean but also explain to the politicians what the politicians mean. And it is part of a solicitor's job to listen to your case and advise you what a judge may decide.

None of this detracts from the role of this book. If it opens up a new avenue of thought which you follow up in a heavy textbook, or enables you to go to your (probably unimaginative and self-protecting) solicitor and say 'Hey, what about doing this?', then it is just as much a success as on those occasions when it alone solves a problem for you. It is the first step, the idea, that is important. And this is primarily a book of ideas: ideas that will not be in a textbook, ideas that your solicitor or accountant might overlook, and some that they will never know.

Paul Jenner, 1979

1

HOW TO MINIMISE RISK AND THE CONSEQUENCES OF FAILURE

In which we consider the degree of protection from risk offered by different business units, their advantages and disadvantages; the dangers of the personal guarantee; the quality of professional advice; and the necessity of thorough research.

A successful businessman has defined his most vital skill as 'taking the risk out of gambling', which says it all. From the first second of the first hour that you plan your enterprise you must search out and eliminate risk as completely as possible.

There is nothing either illegal or immoral or counter-productive in taking a defensive attitude. The law does not require that you should perish along with your business provided you have taken advantage of constructing your operation in a particular way, nor does convention any longer demand that a failed businessman should take a pistol on to the balcony.

Ask yourself the following questions. What will happen to me if my business goes into liquidation? Can my bank proceed against me personally for any losses? Can the creditors? Could I lose my house and everything else that I possess?

Yes?

If you are already in business this chapter will show you what you should have done, and, hopefully, what there is still time to do. If you are starting it will show you how to arrange your affairs so that you can answer 'No' to those last three questions. Do not learn the hard way.

I CHOICE OF BUSINESS UNIT

The full range of business units available to the smaller businessman is as follows:

Liability unlimited	*Liability limited*
Sole proprietorship	Limited partnership
Partnership	Company limited by guarantee
Unlimited company	Private limited company

You will always be either directly or indirectly liable for the debts of your business unless you enjoy limited liability. In a risk situation, unless there is some other overriding consideration (and there are very few), then your basic building block must be the private limited liability company.

The Private Limited Liability Company   *problems 1–11*

The private limited liability company has three important features:

1. The liability of members (shareholders) for the company's debts is limited.

2. The company has a legal personality quite separate from its members.

3. The company has a share capital and the right to transfer shares is restricted.

As the director of a limited company you take on double homework because when liability is limited potential creditors have the right to know to what sum you have limited yourself and what capability your business has of paying them. You have to maintain various registers for public inspection and from information they contain make an annual return to the Registrar of Companies.

The annual return includes a statement of mortgages and charges; a list of members; and particulars of directors and the company secretary. The annual return must be accompanied by the balance sheet; the profit and loss account; and the auditor's and directors' reports.

HOW LIMITED LIABILITY WORKS

When a company limited by shares is formed it is given a nominal capital divided into shares, some or all of which may be issued. Of those issued some or all may be fully paid – that is, the company has received the full issue price. The sum that the shareholder has paid or agreed to pay for his shares is the maximum he can lose *as a shareholder*. (It is common for director/shareholders of private companies to give personal

9

guarantees to banks etc under which additional sums may be lost.) Where the shareholder has only paid part towards the cost of his shares, then, on a winding-up, he may be required to pay what is owing on them.

EXAMPLE: Company X had a share capital of £1,000 and two shareholders who were also directors, each with 500 £1 shares. The first man had paid £500 into the company for his shares but the second only £200. (Nevertheless, he was the legal owner of the shares.) The company borrowed £10,000 from a bank to buy a building plot and the loan was secured by a first mortgage on the land and the work-in-progress. The first man also loaned the company £10,000 to develop the site and his loan was secured by a second charge on the land and work-in-progress. The men voted themselves salaries of £480 a month each.

Materials bought on credit were delivered and the work commenced. On 12 July one supplier delivered a particularly large amount of materials, ordered in good faith and worth over £2,000. On 13 July, which was about six months after the project commenced, the bank called in its loan. The company was unable to repay, the bank appointed a receiver in respect of its mortgage, and the company immediately announced voluntary liquidation. The following sums were outstanding: £10,000 to suppliers, £10,000 plus interest to the bank, £10,000 plus interest to the first man and £700 to the two men as shareholders.

What happened?

The development fetched £21,000, of which the bank received £11,000 – its loan plus interest – because it had a first mortgage. The first man ranked behind the bank, having a second charge, and would have got his £10,000 back in full if it had not been for costs. The only other asset of the company was the £300 owed by the second man on his shares. The liquidator took that for his costs. The ordinary creditors, the suppliers, received nothing on debts of £10,000, as their materials had been taken under the first and second charges, and the shareholders, as shareholders, also received nothing. They could only get their money back after the creditors had been satisfied in full. The supplier who had delivered goods on 12 July complained bitterly: on 11 July the goods were undisputedly his, but on 13 July the company had gone into voluntary liquidation, after which 'his' goods had been sold off and the proceeds given to a director/shareholder, the man 'responsible' for the loss.

The legal case is clear. The goods had been delivered to the company and belonged to the company even though they had not been paid for; the first man was a secured creditor and therefore ahead of the ordinary creditors in the queue. The suppliers had lost their £10,000. As shareholders the two men had lost £500 each but had each drawn £3,000 in salaries.

And no one could touch it.

In legal terms there are natural and artificial persons. You are a natural person; a company is an artificial person, treated in law as if it had an independent life of its own. Except in certain special circumstances, no creditor of a company may sue its shareholders, even though those shareholders may not be protected by limited liability. This is because shareholders and their companies have separate legal personalities.

However, where separate legal personality is enjoyed without limited liability, as in the unlimited company, the shareholders are still liable to the company: the creditor sues the company, which, being unable to pay the sum, is put into liquidation, and the shareholders must then pay into the company whatever sum is necessary to meet the deficit, without ceiling. There is only a ceiling on this liability when liability is limited, as in the limited liability company.

Thus separate legal personality places a shareholder one step away from creditors, but unless a company is limited, then, on a winding-up, ultimate liability remains.

Exceptions to separate legal personality
1. If the membership remains below two (for a public company the number is seven) for six months, the remaining member becomes liable for the company's debts.
2. Where paramount public interest is concerned the courts may rule that the company cannot be considered separately from its members (for example, if a British company were controlled by enemy aliens).
3. The formation of a company will not enable its members to evade their legal obligations as individuals (for example, where a company engages in activities that its members as individuals had contracted not to engage in).
4. If the business is being carried on with intent to defraud, then those responsible or who knew may be held liable for all or

11

any of the company's debts. (For example, if the men in the illustration on p. 10 had ordered the £2,000 of materials knowing that the company was about to go into liquidation unable to meet its debts, they might have been made personally liable.)

SHARES
One aspect of the existence of a share capital is that the greatest say does not necessarily go to the person taking the largest risk. Ten ordinary voting shares can walk all over 100 non-voting preference shares.

The rights to which any particular class of shareholder is entitled are decided, within the given legal framework, by the company. Details for any particular company are contained in its memorandum or articles of association, which must be consulted.

Preference shares
1. A dividend is paid to preference shareholders before any money is paid to other shareholders.
2. Interest is at a fixed rate, calculated on the nominal price of a share.
3. There can be no dividend in a profitless year. (In fact there is no contractual right to any dividend unless the articles so specify.)
4. In the event of a winding-up, preference shareholders have no priority for repayment over ordinary shareholders, unless (as is usual) this is expressly provided. Where there is a surplus, preference shareholders are entitled to a proportion related to the nominal value of their shares only if they have not been given priority for repayment.
5. Preference shares may carry voting rights but are normally non-voting.
6. Cumulative preference shares entitle the holder to back interest unpaid in a profitless year.
7. Redeemable preference shares are the only class of share which the company itself may buy back.

Ordinary shares
1. A dividend is only paid to ordinary shareholders after the full fixed rate of interest has been paid to preference shareholders.
2. Interest is not at a fixed rate, but is set by the company each year in accordance with its performance.

3. There can be no dividend in a profitless year and there is no obligation to pay a dividend in a profitable year. (But, in the case of a close company – basically one with less than five participants or where the shareholders are also the directors – the tax inspector may consider that the non-distribution of distributable profits is a tax dodge and may tax accordingly.)

4. In the event of a winding-up, the memorandum or articles generally provide that ordinary shareholders receive nothing until preference shareholders have been repaid in full; in this case if there is a surplus it will go to the ordinary shareholders. But where preference shareholders have been given no priority for repayment of capital on a winding-up, then the ordinary shareholders will share assets rateably with them.

5. Ordinary shares normally carry voting rights.

6. There is no provision for carrying forward interest that 'ought' to have been paid in a bad year.

7. A company must not deal in its ordinary shares.

Deferred shares

1. A dividend is only paid to deferred shareholders after the full fixed rate of interest has been paid to preference shareholders and a predetermined minimum to ordinary shareholders. Deferred shareholders might then take all the residue, or, more likely, there may be a formula for sharing the residue between the deferred and ordinary shareholders.

2. Interest is not at a fixed rate, but is set by the company each year in accordance with its performance.

3. The company is not obliged to pay a dividend to deferred shareholders.

4. In the event of a winding-up, deferred shares may rank with or behind ordinary shares. In some notable frauds, deferred shares have, however, ranked ahead of other classes.

5. Deferred shares carry extra voting rights (for example, a £1 deferred share may carry one vote and a £5 ordinary share one vote).

6. & 7. As for ordinary shares.

Gearing

The relationship between preference shares and ordinary shares is known as gearing. (The term is also applied to the proportion of shareholders' funds to borrowed money.)

When a company issues more preference than ordinary

shares, then in a poor year the preference shareholders will mop up all the available profit. But in a good year the preference holders still receive the same boring fixed interest, leaving the surplus to a small number of ordinary shareholders who in consequence may receive a spectacular dividend. That is high gearing.

MECHANICS OF FORMATION

The formation of a private limited liability company requires as a minimum a nominal capital of £100; two shareholders; one director; and a company secretary. (An alternative minimum is two directors, one of whom is also company secretary.)

Various documents have to be deposited with and approved by the Registrar of Companies before a Certificate of Incorporation is issued. The most important documents are the memorandum and articles of association.

The memorandum of association

The memorandum deals with the name of the company; its objects and powers; the limitation of liability; and the nominal capital. It also states where the registered office is to be, either 'in England' or 'in Scotland', and within fourteen days of incorporation the actual address must be filed with the Registrar. The registered office is the address to which legal communications may be sent and at which certain registers should be kept for public inspection. These are registers of members; directors and the company secretary; directors' interests in company shares; and charges on company assets. If a company acts beyond its powers as laid down in the memorandum then it is said to act *ultra vires* (see pp. 100–1).

The articles of association

The articles deal with the powers of directors; the frequency of meetings; the method of appointing the board of directors; other management matters; and the breakdown of capital into classes of shares (which may also be dealt with by the memorandum).

Alteration of memorandum and articles

In respect of the memorandum, the company may change its name; change the address of its registered office (but not from England to Scotland or vice versa); become unlimited; or

14

reduce, increase or rearrange its share capital. It may also change its object on three main grounds: to enable the company to carry on its business more efficiently; to enable the company to pursue its main object by better methods; or to enable the company to carry on a complementary activity.

The company may alter or add to its articles by special resolution, but the articles must remain consistent with the memorandum and where there is a conflict between the two documents the memorandum wins.

The Other Business Units

THE COMPANY LIMITED BY GUARANTEE
If you wish to form an (intentionally) non-profit-making body, consider the company limited by guarantee, where you do not have to contribute risk (share) capital at the outset, only in a deficit situation on a winding-up.

The company limited by guarantee has the following features:

1. The liability of members is limited to that amount which in the memorandum they guarantee to contribute to the company's debts on a winding-up. The guarantee is not an asset of the company (issued shares are); it is a contingent liability on members.

2. The company has a legal personality quite separate from its members.

3. The company may have a share capital, but this is unusual.

THE LIMITED PARTNERSHIP
If you wish to invest in a partnership as a sleeping partner the limited partnership should be considered, but conversion to a limited company is probably better.

The limited partnership has the following features:

1. It has at least one unlimited partner.

2. It has at least one partner whose liability for debts of the partnership is limited to the amount that he contributes on becoming a partner.

3. There is no separate legal personality.

4. Limited partners can take no active part in management; general partners have complete control. (As a result of this a

limited partner's income must be taxed as 'unearned'.)

5. Various details have to be filed with the Registrar of Companies, including the names of unlimited partners; the names of limited partners and the amount they have contributed; and the term of the partnership.

See also 'The partnership' below.

THE UNLIMITED COMPANY

If you want your affairs to be kept private and you need separate legal personality but not limited liability, consider the unlimited company.

The unlimited company has the following features:

1. The liability of members is not limited.

2. The company has a legal personality quite separate from its members.

3. The company may or may not have a share capital.

4. Accounts do not have to be filed with the Registrar of Companies. (This privilege does not apply in the case of subsidiaries of limited companies.)

THE PARTNERSHIP   *problems 12–15*

Beware of partnerships, not only for the difficulties that may arise between partners and third parties but for those that will arise among partners. Solicitors, who should know best, may use partnerships, but then, for ethical reasons, they are denied limited liability.

The partnership has the following features:

1. The liability of members is not limited.

2. The partnership does not have a legal personality separate from its members. A feature of this is that a creditor may single out and sue an individual partner. (For convenience actions may be brought against partnerships by name, nevertheless it is the partners who are being sued.)

3. There can be no share capital.

4. Accounts are private.

The rights and responsibilities of partners are laid down by the Partnership Act 1890 and will always apply unless modified by the partnership agreement. Every partner has a right to participate in management (unless a sleeping partner); has a veto on major decisions, such as the admission of a new partner; must contribute to losses in proportion to his share in the partnership; and is generally only liable for debts incurred while actually a member of the partnership.

Formation can be either by signed, sealed and delivered document; by written partnership agreement; by oral agreement; or inferred by the court from behaviour in the event of a legal dispute. Partners trading under a name other than a combination of their own names must apply to the Registrar of Business Names.

THE SOLE PROPRIETORSHIP

In non-risk situations *only*, you, as a sole owner, should consider the sole proprietorship.

The sole proprietorship has the following features:

1. The liability of the businessman for the debts of the business is without limit.

2. The business and the businessman have the same legal personality and, therefore, a judgement against the business is, in fact, a judgement against the businessman, affecting his personal credit rating.

3. There can be no share capital.

The sole proprietor wishing to trade under a title other than his own name must apply to the Registrar of Business Names. This is the only formation requirement and the business is continued with a similar lack of formality which, in non-risk situations, is its advantage over the limited company. Accounts are private and do not have to be audited. There are no annual returns, no registers, and no objects clauses in a memorandum to be observed.

At the time of writing there is tax relief for individuals carrying on their trade partly abroad and against previous income for individuals who make a loss in the first three years of setting up a new business.

II PERSONAL COLLATERAL AND THE COMPANY LOAN

What the law giveth, the bank taketh away.

You form your private limited liability company. It needs finance. You ask your bank. Your bank asks you to sign away the limit on your liability in respect of their loan.

Now if an ordinary trade creditor asks for a personal guarantee, you tell him to take his business elsewhere. There are plenty more where he came from. But the bank is one creditor who makes you an offer you cannot refuse. By signing a personal guarantee for them in respect of a company loan, you undertake that if your company cannot repay then you will. One stroke of the pen and you increase the consequences of failure. The bank may ask you to allow a specific charge on a personal asset. If the company cannot repay they sell it to recover their money, and their favourite asset is your house. Your home.

You don't think it's right? What has right to do with anything? The banks are merely doing what you would be equally well advised to do – seeking out and eliminating risk. You must get it out of your mind that the major banks are, like the Church, institutions that can do no wrong. The banks maintain that image of strength and integrity to put the frighteners on you. But once you begin to see them as ordinary commercial undertakings out to make money you can fight them.

Well at least try. It's not immoral.

THE PERSONAL GUARANTEE   *problems 16, 17*

The bank view of the personal guarantee is that it is security; it is a sign of good faith; and it keeps the guarantor committed to the project. It follows, therefore, that if a company gets into difficulty and the guarantor is at pains to be seen doing everything possible to protect the bank's interests and fully co-operates with the bank, then the bank may consider that the businessman has already gone a long way towards discharging his obligations under the guarantee. He has fulfilled two of the three objectives. The bank may be lenient over the third.

Thus a businessman who gives a personal guarantee for a £100,000 loan made to one of his companies may be asked to contribute only a fairly nominal sum to a loss of, say, £50,000 on that loan. An offer of £5,000 cash might satisfy the bank.

According to one senior bank executive, 'Banks today are coming to regard the personal guarantee more as a way of binding the guarantor to the project than as security for the loan. Banks are tending not to enforce guarantees to the full amount where the borrower has acted honestly with the bank.' However, policy changes from year to year and from bank to bank, so this attitude cannot be relied upon.

18

A guarantee must be evidenced in writing; the consideration is generally the creditor's lending to the debtor (see Chapter Five on contract).

If you are a co-guarantor you will normally be asked to sign a *joint and several* guarantee, which means that all the guarantors may be sued jointly or individually, and if you alone settle with the bank you may claim equalising sums from your co-sureties. A guarantor who pays in full may take over any securities given to the bank by the debtor. Unless the guarantee provides otherwise, a guarantor may be discharged if the bank releases a co-surety or if there is a material alteration of the original agreement between debtor and creditor without the consent of the guarantor, including the release of securities given by the debtor. No guarantee exists where the principal debtor has been released or cannot be held liable – if, for example, he is a minor.

SPECIFIC PERSONAL SECURITY

The bank view of a charge on your house or any other personal asset is that it is solely for security, and thus, in contrast to the case of the personal guarantee which is considered to have other functions as well, the bank will always proceed against a specific charge to the maximum of their loss. If you charge your house to the bank and something goes wrong, then (unless, of course, you can come up with the money from somewhere else) you have lost it.

III PEOPLE AND RESEARCH

SOLICITORS   *problem 18*

Choose a solicitor for his predilection to uphold the letter of the law when it is in your interest, rather than the spirit; the spirit when it is in your interest, rather than the letter. He must be ruthless enough to exploit the loopholes that will enable you to defeat the intentions of those who framed the law; ruthless enough to manipulate the awful slowness of the legal process to your advantage. Above all, look for a man with good practical sense as well as a knowledge of the theory.

As you have more time to meditate on your own problems than your solicitor does, you should not neglect to look for a solution yourself. Consult books. Begin with this one. Then go on to the thick ones that set out every detail and nuance of the law. (A little knowledge may be a dangerous thing but it is still better than none at all.) When you have done that you may not only know more than your own solicitor, you may know more than your opponent's solicitor. And that is important, because a curious fact about solicitors, until you find the very best, is that an opponent's solicitor is always better than your own.

Once you have some ideas for a solution to your problems you can put them to your solicitor. Think of him as a sounding board, as a clerk to deal with routine and as a guide through the labyrinth of legal procedures. Then you will not be disappointed. If his advice differs from your own view, do not be afraid to back your own judgement. You may have greater insight.

Occasionally, it may pay to keep your solicitor a little in the dark about your intentions. For example, you may wish to bluff your opponents that you are prepared to go to court when in fact you are not, and your solicitor may act with more conviction if he does not know you are bluffing.

Always confirm your instructions to your solicitor in writing. One of the reasons for having a solicitor is not that he will avoid mistakes which left to your own devices you would have made, but that when he does make them you can at least attempt to get redress from him. If you have nothing in writing you have little hope.

ACCOUNTANTS   *problem 19*

Many accountants are little more than glorified bookkeepers. If you are in a small business this may not worry you. What should worry you in company situations, where your accountant will also be your auditor, is finding a man who has the ability to hold a telescope to a blind eye.

The accounts of your companies can be presented quite legitimately in a number of different ways. You want them presented your way, not the Chancellor's.

BANK MANAGERS   *problem 20*

Never bank at a sub-branch. The manager there carries little weight with his superiors. In particular if he is well past middle age and newly appointed, you can be sure his bosses had kindly regard for the size of his retirement pension rather than his ability. But do not bank either at a main branch where you only get to see the under-manager.

Find out what limit the manager can go to on his own authority. It may be worth banking at a central London main branch where the manager can personally authorise, say, £25,000. The local main branch manager may be able to go to £10,000 but a sub-branch manager only to £5,000 or less.

Whatever bank advertising may say, forget the manager as a source of advice about your business. But he is a source of information on his own business: the personality of the area manager, the attitude of the bank on different types of loan, the criteria used for assessing projects etc.

Make sure you find a manager you hit it off with on a personal level. And that does not mean someone with a weak personality over whom you think you can exert some influence; he will never have the guts to back you unreservedly to his superiors. You need someone confident in his own judgement and a little aggressive, and that often rules out the younger man.

Always:

1. Appear to be straightforward with your manager.

2. Keep in regular contact when you have a loan. (No news is suspicious news.)

3. Fulfil commitments exactly. (If you ask for a bridging loan to be repaid on 14 March then repay it on 14 March – even if you have to borrow from someone else to do it.)

Your reputation is worth money at a bank. One day you may need to cash it in.

RESEARCH   *problem 21*

An examination of some famous careers shows the benefit of good groundwork.

EXAMPLES:

(a) Bernard Cornfeld was the mastermind behind the Investors Overseas Services, the most meteoric mutual fund ever. But he started in 1953 only as a salesman for Walter Benedick's Investors Planning Corporation. It was not until 1960 that Cornfeld incorporated his own company.

(b) John Bentley began as a £17-a-week stockbroker's analyst. His training and experience there enabled him to spot the Scottish Life situation, which he took to Jim Slater.

(c) Nigel Broackes inherited £25,000, invested it in property conversions – and lost most of it. Only then did Broackes, now boss of Trafalgar House, take the £25-a-week job with an estate agent that enabled him to spot the Collins & Collins & Rawlence deal.

(d) Harry Hyams went to work for Joe Levy's estate agency in 1945 at the age of seventeen. From there he went to Hamptons, then to Dudley Samuel Harrison, then back to Hamptons. Not until 1959 did he buy the company in Oldham that was to make him famous – or, perhaps, infamous.

These four men all had one thing in common: research preceded success – in their case research by experience. And that experience was generally obtained at the expense of somebody else – often the best way.

PROBLEMS AND SOLUTIONS

1. I am in business on my own but would like to enjoy limited liability.
A minimum of two people is required for a private limited liability company – two shareholders, one a director, the other company secretary. Give one share to your wife, father, son or some other suitable person and make that person company secretary. Issue more than one share to yourself to have control at shareholders' meetings.

2. I need to form a private limited liability company urgently.
Telephone a company registration service and they will be able to offer you companies, which they have kept dormant since incorporation, for your type of business. This will save you several weeks. You will be obliged to accept the name, memorandum and articles as filed although you may subsequently make certain changes (see 'Alteration of memorandum and articles', pp. 14–15). Cost 'off-the-shelf' is about £80 at the time of writing for a company with a nominal capital of £100.

3. The Registrar of Companies has turned down my choice of name.
The Registrar may refuse titles that would incorrectly associate the company with charities; that give a misleading impression of size or importance; that improperly include the words 'Bank' or 'Investment Trust' or 'Building Society' or 'Co-operative';

that include the name of someone unconnected with the company; that suggest royal or government connection; or that resemble the title of an existing company. Use of the name of a director or shareholder does not guarantee acceptance. Consult the Registrar before submitting a new name or buy 'off-the-shelf' (see above).

4. Confusion is arising between my company and another formed recently with a similar name.

If yours is the 'genuine' business you may obtain an injunction preventing the new company from using the name, provided that you can satisfy the court that the new company's name is so similar to yours as to cause confusion and either that it is carrying on a business similar to your own or that it is obtaining business as a result of customers assuming that it is your company or associated with it. The courts will not prevent an *individual* carrying on business in his own name even if this does give rise to confusion.

5. What share capital should I have?

The minimum possible is a nominal capital of £100 and an issued capital of two £1 shares. A large issued capital gives substance to a company, impresses banks and makes it easier to borrow. But issued capital is risk capital and fairly permanent, so it seems foolish to risk more than necessary.

6. I have invested £25,000 share capital in my company. I now consider this sum excessive.

The court may agree to repayment of capital where a company has cut back and disposed of assets or where shares carry fixed interest above the market rate (enabling the company to borrow more cheaply), but only if it is satisfied that creditors will not be defrauded.

7. I am a 50 per cent shareholder in a private limited company. The other shareholder intends to transfer half his holding to his wife against my wishes.

Details of the restrictions on share transfers in private companies are contained in the articles of association: consult. The articles may empower directors to refuse transfers on certain grounds or provide that a member must first offer his shares to existing members. However, it is unusual for there to be a restriction on transfers to wives/husbands, so you will probably have to persuade or pressure.

8. I hold 9 per cent preference shares in a private company but last year received no dividend.

The preference shareholder only has a contractual right to a dividend in a profitable year if the articles so specify. If they do not but the company has made sufficient profit in the year in question you may be able to take action against the directors for oppression, as you might if the directors have deliberately concealed profits. If there is no profit, there can be no dividend; if there is a loss, then worry about more than your dividend.

9. A limited company in which I am a shareholder has been defrauded by a customer but the directors are taking no action.

Your remedy lies in gaining the support of other shareholders to compel the company to take action because in *Foss* v. *Harbottle* (1843) it was held that where a company has been defrauded, the plaintiff in an action must be the company itself, not an individual shareholder or group of shareholders. But if you suspect that the refusal to act is itself fraudulent (because the directors have conspired with the debtor), then other remedies are application to the courts or the Department of Trade, or, in a winding-up, misfeasance proceedings. Also in a winding-up the rule of *Foss* v. *Harbottle* may be suspended.

10. Some business acquaintances formed a company to do house-building and I took up shares. Now they say house-building is not profitable and intend entering areas in which I do not want to retain an investment.

Modern drafting of the objects clause of the memorandum of association provides for a wide range of activities. An action to prevent the company entering new areas is, therefore, unlikely to succeed unless it be an area not mentioned at all in the objects clause or unless there were highly specific objects laid down, such as the development of particular sites. Try to pressure the other shareholders into buying you out.

11. I have been brought a manufacturing proposition that fits

24

in rather well with our present activities and could double our profits, but it is risky.

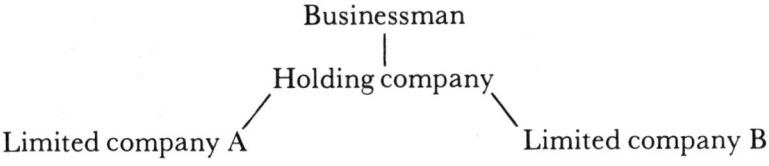

Businessman
|
Holding company

Limited company A   Limited company B

Above is one arrangement for protecting company A, your existing company, from possible losses in the new venture by putting the new manufacturing proposition into company B. The holding company will not trade and, therefore, runs no risk of insolvency but combines the profits of A and B if the latter is successful.

12. I agreed to accept a share of the profits of a firm in settlement of money owed. Now the firm is in difficulty and some creditors are alleging that I am a partner.
Under the Partnership Act 1890 it may be inferred that anyone receiving a share of the profits of a partnership is a partner. You must demonstrate that this arrangement is purely for the settlement of a debt.

13. I am owed money by a partnership for goods that were delivered several months ago.
Partners are jointly liable for their firm's contracts and it is a feature of this type of liability that you may sue all the partners jointly or any individual partner. But bear in mind that you have only one right of action and if you follow the latter course and successfully sue one partner and he is unable to pay you, right to obtain satisfaction from the other partners has nevertheless been forfeited. Thus, while the threat to sue one individual partner may be a useful lever, it is normal practice to sue all the partners together.

Note that had you been bringing an action for tort – for example, for negligence – then the partners would have been *jointly and severally* liable and you would have had the right to sue each partner successively or all the partners jointly.

14. I wish to retire from a partnership. How can I ensure that I

am not held liable for debts any longer and how can I capitalise on my partnership share?

You will remain liable for all debts incurred while a partner, unless all parties affected agree to a contract of novation. Advertise your retirement in the *London Gazette* and inform all existing suppliers to ensure that you are not held liable for debts incurred after you ceased to be a partner. As regards the second part of your question you should consult your partnership agreement if you have one. You may be able to give notice of the dissolution of the partnership so that the assets may be sold. But if the main asset is goodwill this might not be wise. You can always assign your share of the partnership profits but the assignee will not become a partner unless your other partners agree. You could become a sleeping (limited?) partner and draw income. Finally, your existing partners may buy you out.

15. A partner in a firm ordered goods from me, which I supplied. Now his partners say he was not authorised to place the order and are returning the goods.

Provided that you were not aware that he was not so authorised and that he acted within his apparent authority, then his order is binding on his partners as regards yourself (although he may be liable to his partners over the abuse). But you should examine closely the genuine motive behind the cancellation; it may be that the partnership is in financial difficulty, in which case it may be in your best interest to accept the goods back.

16. I simply cannot get an overdraft for my company unless I also give a personal guarantee. How can I protect myself?

The first step is to make the bank take a general charge over the company. They may do this anyway, but in many cases they will not bother where the personal covenant looks adequate.

EXAMPLE:

Company assets	*Company liabilities*
£25,000	Bank £20,000
	Trade £30,000
	£50,000

In this situation if the bank has no general charge it will get only two-fifths of the £25,000 assets and look to you for its remaining £10,000. With a general charge the bank can recover all of its £20,000 from the company, leaving £5,000 for other creditors.

The second step is to try to have the guarantee limited to a specific amount rather than for all monies owing. The reason for this is that if the facility creeps above the guarantee limit you cannot be asked for the additional amount.

Get the lowest rate of true interest possible, and always make maximum use of the credit available from suppliers.

Finally, if the project goes badly finish it, if possible, before the bank's loan exceeds the company's resources.

17. My bank are suing me under a personal guarantee. Could there be a loophole?

With regard to the actual document, there are unlikely to be any technical grounds on which a personal guarantee to a major bank could be invalidated. The big banks have been using them too long to make mistakes. However, it is always possible that there will be some flaw in a guarantee prepared by a fringe bank as they have not had the same number of years to perfect the document.

Chapter Five deals with the law of contract; see in particular the case of *Lloyds Bank Ltd* v. *Bundy* (1975) on pp. 102–3.

18. My solicitor acted for me in the purchase of a building plot, yet I now discover I have no access as another company owns a 'ransome strip' cutting off my land from the road.

It will not be easy but you will have to consider suing your solicitor. He is insured. Discuss this with him if you have not already done so. There may be some right to an easement that you have overlooked. Perhaps you can twist his arm for the cost of purchasing an easement without recourse to the courts.

19. The auditor charged a fortune to certify the accounts last year.

An auditor's work, and therefore his remuneration, will be reduced considerably if you keep the books correctly and file invoices etc systematically for easy verification. You can save on accountancy charges by preparing your own accounts, which the auditor will then investigate and certify.

20. My bank has agreed to an overdraft facility and my bank manager has virtually guaranteed that the money will not be called in for two years. Can I rely upon that?

No. In the right circumstances you may view it as a probability;

it is not a certainty. Bank managers are only human. Do not make the mistake of attributing to them superhuman moral standards.

21. How can I find out about the profitability of an area of business I am considering?

Examine the accounts of existing companies filed with the Registrar. You can do this at Companies House in either London or Cardiff on payment of a small sum per company file. You might also consult the Department of Trade, trade associations etc. You will then have to go on to produce budgets, cash flows etc of your own (see Chapter Three). As you appear to lack experience in this field, you will have to gain some without risk, possibly working for someone else; or you will have to bring in experts.

USEFUL BOOKS AND ADDRESSES

Charlesworth, J. (ed. T. E. Cain), *Principles of Company Law* (Stevens, 1968)

Chorley, Lord, and P. E. Smart, *Leading Cases in the Law of Banking* (Sweet & Maxwell, 1977)

Drake, Charles D., *Partnership Law* (Sweet & Maxwell, 1972)

Gower, L. C. B., *Principles of Modern Company Law* (Stevens, 1969)

Underhill, Sir A. (ed. E. R. Hardy Ivamy), *Principles of the Law of Partnership* (10th ed., Butterworth, 1975)

To investigate or register a company: Companies House, Crown Way, Maindy, Cardiff CF4 3UZ. And in London: Companies House, 55 City Road, London EC1Y 1BB

For information about the home market: Department of Trade, 1 Victoria Street, London SW1H 0ET

For information about export markets: Export House, 50 Ludgate Hill, London EC4M 7HU

For company formation services see Yellow Pages (Company Promoters) or your solicitor or accountant.

2
FINANCE

In which we consider how to reduce dependence on borrowed money; and how and where to borrow money.

There are people with money to invest. Some put it into pension schemes with insurance companies, some into building societies, some into merchant banks or their own clearing bank, and some put it directly into business, either their own or someone else's. Wherever they place the money they expect interest, and the institution which pays them must get a higher return on the money than the investor. In the case of banks this means that the more money that is deposited with them the more they must lend. If a substantial proportion of their deposits lies idle their margins fall. They may even make a loss. They also make a loss if they re-lend carelessly. So each type of institution works to its own set of rules designed to keep it on the tightrope.

All this is obvious, but it is comforting to think about it.

You just have to find the source whose rules suit your project, and you have to present your project in such a way that the source can see clearly that your proposition and their rules match. Sometimes you will have to redesign to tie in with those rules, and that is where the skill comes in.

But remember that borrowed money is expensive. It is retail. To maximise profit you must minimise bank borrowing, and that is an aim the bank, too, will share. They want to see that your business is making maximum use of its own resources.

I HOW TO MANIPULATE RESOURCES

Methods of reducing dependence on borrowed money include obtaining generous credit from suppliers; giving less credit to customers; stock control (see Chapter Three, V, and problems 28 and 29); increasing profits; reducing taxation; and sale and leaseback.

There is an old joke which runs: 'It's not true to say there is no freedom of speech in this country. You can say anything you like. Once.'

Anyone, also, can obtain lengthy credit. Once. But if you want to stay in business for any length of time without running out of suppliers, some more satisfactory method of obtaining credit must be found than simply ignoring statements and writs. Neither should you send a cheque unsigned; send a cheque undated; send a cheque in which the words and figures disagree; or send a remittance advice but 'forget' to enclose the cheque. These are common techniques which the greenest businessman will recognise for what they are. Sending a cheque undated is ineffective anyway because it is quite proper for the payee to insert a date.

When an order is placed, try something on these lines:

'At this time of year I know you will have to warehouse these goods for two or three months. Why not let me take delivery now, in May, but date the invoice as August? You will still be getting the money just as quickly as if you sold the goods in three months' time with prompt payment. What's more, if I can get started on these goods now I feel confident that I will be able to take a further delivery shortly. You have nothing to lose except clutter in your warehouse and we can both gain.'

When payment is overdue:

'We've been doing business for some time but I haven't had the pleasure of speaking to you until now. You will probably be aware that we have received a reminder from you this week for £1,000 for goods delivered approximately eight weeks ago. I thought I had better telephone you and let you know our situation. Well, I say "our situation", but it's almost universal. You know how things are yourself – you're pressing your customers for payment and we're pressing ours and so on. At the moment I'm afraid to say that our cash flow is a little bit naughty. Things are rather tight and I'm afraid I don't think I'm going to be able to meet this payment for another six weeks. But I can promise you most definitely that I will settle this account without fail by 30 June at the latest, and sooner if I can.'

So far everything is friendly. By keeping in touch with the creditor you have kept the situation cool. You will probably arrive at an amicable compromise. And it is important to be amicable because a businessman who will write off £200 may chase £20 at great expense simply because the debtor has been rude to him.

The creditor compromises for the sake of good business relations and because he knows that to go to court is expensive and will take longer than the time you are asking for.

Dealing with Debtors *problems 26, 27*

Just as you want longer credit from your suppliers so your customers want longer credit from you. This you cannot possibly permit, without some very compelling reason.

CREDIT CONTROL POLICY

You must formulate a policy on credit control, setting out for each customer not only the length of time that will *in practice* be allowed for settlement before business is disrupted by a grade three demand or a writ, but also the amount of credit. This latter will be determined by past experience; a credit rating obtained through the bank; trade references; and the salesman's report. You should also bear in mind that writs for sums exceeding £2,000 will have to be pursued through the High Court, where justice is often dispensed more slowly than in the County Court.

Where you have a large number of customers, standardised demands may be preprinted to accompany statements. Those prepared by you are likely to be more effective than commercial mass-produced stickers to which debtors have become immune.

DISCOUNTS

The possible advantages of offering settlement discounts are that they encourage early settlement and that they give conformity with competitors where there is a standard practice for an industry. But paradoxically, a possible disadvantage is that they may discourage reasonable settlement, and a certain one is cost.

EXAMPLES:

(a) A company that settles within seven days receives a discount of $3\frac{3}{4}$ per cent. If a company that does not settle within seven days wishes to remain competitive with that company, then it must delay its payment until the consequent saving on interest charges compensates. That may take three months.

(b) A company offers a settlement discount of seven days $3\frac{3}{4}$ per cent, which encourages payment four weeks earlier than otherwise. The company has an overdraft at 1 per cent a month, and the cost to the company is therefore $2\frac{3}{4}$ per cent – possibly enough, if saved, to raise profits by a quarter.

Settlement discounts can never encourage companies with cash flow problems; companies without cash flow problems will generally settle in reasonable time anyway. And major customers may dictate their own terms.

EXAMPLE: P—— Ltd obtained an order from a major London store and invoiced the goods on terms of seven days 2 per cent, thirty days net. The store settled after five weeks and took 5 per cent.

DEBT COLLECTORS

The advantage of using a firm of debt collectors used to be that their title was so intimidating that debtors paid up on receipt of their first letter. Today it can only be said in favour of debt collectors that they remove the burden of chasing debts from the principal. They often have a standard procedure which can be time-wasting and they lack the flexibility of approach that the principal can bring to bear. They also cost money.

PERSONAL CONTACT

The telephone demand is more effective than either your written demands or your debt collector's. Staff get to know that the boss is being chased for money. They get anxious about their jobs. And that makes the boss anxious. The telephone call is also a sign that matters have reached a serious-stage and therefore the majority of debtors will respond.

The personal visit has even more nuisance value than the telephone call, and few people are tough enough to resist when face to face with a creditor. The ultimate is to visit a director of the debtor company at his private address.

FURTHER ACTION

If the debtor has refused all demands for payment you may sue him; petition for a winding-up under Section 223 of the Companies Act 1948; take the goods back if possible; or do nothing.

Manipulating Resources — Debtors and Creditors

£000s	Month 1	Month 2	Month 3
Opening balance (OD)*	10	15	17
Payments out	5	6	7
Receipts	0	4	6
Closing balance (OD)*	15	17	18

The above is a cash flow diagram showing the bank overdraft at the beginning (opening balance) and end (closing balance) of the month after allowing for the payments out and receipts shown. But if you delay settling accounts one month longer and induce customers to settle with you one month earlier the effects are dramatic:

£000s	Month 1	Month 2	Month 3
Opening balance (OD)*	10	8	8
Payments out	1	5	6
Receipts	3	5	6
Closing balance (OD)*	8	8	8

The required bank overdraft is cut by £10,000.　　　* overdrawn

The required bank overdraft is cut by £10,000.

Taxation

CORPORATION TAX   *problem 30*

It is the duty of every director of a company to ensure that his company avoids corporation tax as far as possible. To do otherwise is to defraud creditors and shareholders.

The duties of an auditor are laid down in the articles of association or in his contract. If both of these are lacking he is bound only by the specific rules laid down by the Companies Acts and upon these he will arrive at a profit figure and, eventually, liability for corporation tax.

A company is obliged to keep such records as shall 'with reasonable accuracy, at any time, [disclose] the financial position of the company at that time' in accordance with the Companies Act 1976. In particular where a company deals in goods there should be 'statements of stock' held by the company at the end of each financial year; 'statements of stocktakings' from which the 'statements of stock' were prepared; and statements 'in sufficient detail to enable the goods and the buyers and sellers to be identified', unless the company is a retailer.

How are these stocks valued?

The auditor must obtain a certificate stating the amount and value of stock from an officer of the company. He need not investigate further, providing the certificate agrees with the company's stock records (as above) and books. In practice auditors normally make random checks on stocks or make or supervise the stocktaking themselves, but the auditor is not bound by law physically to check that the company possesses the stocks shown by its records, nor need he even value the stocks himself.

EXAMPLE: *Kingston Cotton Mills Co* (1896). It was held that the auditor was not wrong to accept a certificate even though the company's books showed that the prices recently obtained for the products were below those put on the stocks.

Notwithstanding the above, the rules today are framed with the intention of preventing the inflation of profits and therefore the businessman has the auditor on his side when he takes a conservative, even an ultra-conservative, view. Thus, for many companies the simplest method of avoiding corporation tax is to write down stocks; but be warned that carried to an extreme undervaluing stocks amounts to evasion, which is illegal. (The presentation of figures is dealt with in Chapter Three.)

Partnerships and sole proprietorships are not obliged to have their accounts audited.

Sale and Leaseback   *problems 31, 32*

Sale and leaseback is the disposal of freehold premises occupied and owned by a company which then continues to occupy the premises on a long lease. Exceptionally, long-lease rather than freehold properties might be involved.

The advantages are as follows:

1. Money is released for more profitable employment in the business.

2. More money is raised, initially more cheaply than by mortgage, because commercial mortgages are generally for

only 65 per cent of valuation; a purchaser will accept a lower return than a mortgagor because of the compensating capital appreciation of the freehold; and there are no capital repayments.

3. When interest rates are low the value of the freehold as an investment is likely to exceed its value vacant.

4. The lease may itself acquire value.

The disadvantages are as follows:

1. It may be more profitable to leave the money in the freehold than to invest it in the business.

2. Capital appreciation of the freehold is lost.

3. Succeeding rent reviews will eventually cause the rental to exceed the mortgage repayments for a corresponding figure.

4. Rent has to be paid forever; mortgage repayments are for a fixed term.

5. Tax on capital gains. Albeit that there may have been no increase in the value of the premises in real terms, nevertheless tax is levied on the illusory increase taking 1965 as the base year.

EXAMPLE: For a factory purchased in 1950, tax is assessed on the difference between 1965 value and the sale price. The 1965 value may be estimated by proportion or by an expert opinion. For a factory purchased from 1965 onwards, tax is assessed on the difference between the actual purchase and sale prices. Costs of the sale may be taken into account.

FINDING AN INVESTOR

Investment in factories and warehouses has always been considered risky; manufacturers have a habit of becoming insolvent, and retailers are no better. Investors therefore seek a high yield; a strong covenant – that is, an occupier of substance; premises that can be re-let easily if the occupier should be wound up – and that means premises suitable for a variety of trades; and personal guarantees from director/shareholders – which should be resisted.

Smaller premises have always been avoided by the big institutions in their search for strong covenants, but this is changing. Recession has shown itself no respecter of size. This will help to keep the market in smaller investments healthy whenever interest rates come right.

If you decide that the advantages of sale and leaseback outweigh the many disadvantages – and this is most often the case in takeover situations – then try approaching estate agents – they often have good contacts for this; family and investment trusts; property investment companies; insurance companies; and pension funds. Also advertise: the *Estates Gazette* is recommended.

II HOW TO MANIPULATE SOURCES

In 1972 it was easy to borrow money. In 1975 it was not easy to borrow money. In 1972 you could obtain 100 per cent finance on property deals. In 1975 you could obtain only 65 per cent if you could obtain any at all.

Timing, as in all things, is important in the manipulation of sources. Don't they say you have to be in the right place at the right time?

You meet businessmen and read about businessmen who claim they started with nothing. And you have nothing. How then do you begin?

The First Loan

1. Personal collateral. A first charge on your house is a very acceptable security to your bank. A second charge is almost as good provided there is adequate cover for the bank after the building society.

2. Friends and relatives. If you can borrow from this source but still need a commercial loan, you will not be able to allow your friends any security as this will diminish your ability to borrow from other sources.

3. Friendly sources. It may be that because of your contacts or relationship with a company, you will be able to obtain a loan where otherwise you might fail.

EXAMPLE: Bernard Cornfeld's stake to begin Investors Overseas Services was $26,000 borrowed from the Dreyfus Corporation for whom he was a successful dealer.

4. Team up. While you have ideas and expertise but no access to funds it may be that you can join forces with someone who has access.

EXAMPLES:

(a) Nigel Broackes's finance for the Collins & Collins &

Rawlence deal was arranged by family stockbroking friend David Fremantle.

(b) During the early seventies C——— Securities Ltd operated as financiers. They took a half share in property deals for which they arranged 100 per cent finance by multiplying a small cash stake of their own with a clearing bank loan.

5. Participation. The prime financial source puts up 100 per cent backing for a major share in the project. This is inevitably a controlling share and it may go well beyond that.

EXAMPLES:

(a) John Bentley discovered the Scottish Life situation (control for £3 million of assets worth three times the book valuation of £35 million) and took it to Jim Slater. Slater set the deal up and Bentley received £50,000, virtually a commission, plus Slater's participating backing for further deals.

(b) A small family building company, C——— M——— Ltd, agreed to buy two ¾-acre building plots at £15,000 each. One hundred per cent finance for both purchase and development was put up by a fringe bank which formed a joint company with the builders in which it held 51 per cent of the shares.

6. Sell-out. Where you fail to arrange any finance for a deal because you lack either substance or experience it may still be possible to make some money for it by introducing it to someone else.

EXAMPLES:

(a) P——— W——— invented a toy but was unable to get any backing as he had no manufacturing experience and no capital of his own. He finally arranged for an established toy manufacturer to produce his invention and pay him a royalty.

(b) G——— D——— Ltd contracted to buy a 3-acre building site with a six-month completion date. Being unable to raise finance in that time they allowed another development company to complete the purchase in return for a commission.

Types of Loan   *problems 33–40*

The *overdraft* is the normal clearing bank loan. The borrower is given a maximum facility on his current account but only uses such part of it as is necessary at a given time. The overdraft is constantly rising and falling as payments are made and the receipts banked (you can see this effect in the cash flows in Part I of this chapter and in the next chapter), and for this reason interest is calculated on a day-to-day basis. All clearing bank loans are repayable on demand but overdrafts are more repayable on demand than other loans.

The rules of the overdraft in an ongoing situation are simple. Like all rules they can be broken but it helps to stay within them. The overdraft should be repaid entirely at some point each year even if it is to be renewed or even increased the following year. The cash flow projection should, therefore, show the account in credit at some time and should look at worst neutral over twelve months and preferably positive. All this gives the bank confidence that the borrower could repay if the overdraft had to be called in unexpectedly. The bank likes to see plenty of action in the account; it likes to see the facility fully utilised from time to time and it gets worried if the overdraft sticks around the same figure, especially if it sticks around the top.

The clearers are in a unique position to monitor their client's activities because, unless the customer is handling cash under the counter, the monies that mirror his performance flow through the current account. But while the non-clearers do not offer a current account and overdraft as such, they may nevertheless tailor their advances and mop up receipts so as to retain some control over their money. It is rare for a substantial sum of money for working capital to be loaned to a small businessman as a lump for him to administer at his own discretion. For example, a merchant bank loan to a building company might be advanced in stages as work progresses, paid directly to the client's clearing bank account, and the merchant bank might insist upon the building company's solicitor paying the receipts from house sales directly to them. Thus, the amount outstanding to the merchant bank at any time would fluctuate as with an overdraft.

The businessman seeking a *non-overdraft loan* should not grab at the first offer of money but should negotiate over structure; it may be important. As we have seen, the loan may be made as a lump sum or advanced in stages as a project progresses. It may be for a fixed term and repayable in predetermined stages; for a fixed term and repayable at the end of the period; for the duration of a certain project or projects and repayable out of the proceeds as they arise; or for the duration of a certain project or projects and repayable upon completion. The rate of interest may be fixed for the duration and, where the term is known, cal-

38

culated in advance and added to the regular capital repayments. Alternatively, the interest rate may fluctuate with bank or finance house base rates; in that case the interest charge either becomes payable in cash quarterly, six-monthly or yearly, or is debited quarterly, six-monthly or yearly and rolled up so that repayments of interest are made simultaneously with repayments of capital. The businessman should be well aware that when he enjoys the convenience of having interest charges rolled up he is, of course, paying interest on interest, which can get expensive.

The easiest type of loan to organise should be the *back-to-back bridge*. But the bridge more often than not goes hand in hand with speculation and the banks have been taught by successive governments that they must disapprove of speculation. So the bridge is financially easy but politically difficult. Not too difficult, however, for T—— T—— Ltd, who contracted to buy a piece of land for £20,000 and simultaneously exchanged contracts to sell it on for £30,000. The completion date negotiated for the resale was unfortunately two months after the latest date for completion of the purchase by T—— T—— Ltd, who had only £5,000. A clearing bank put up the necessary £15,000. The money loaned was a bridge, because it bridged two transactions; and it was back-to-back because the bank had a guaranteed takeout from the sell-on, barring accident.

In the *open-ended situation* the bank steps in with finance to bridge the gap between one certain transaction and one uncertain transaction. For example, when S—— M—— Ltd took over B—— Ltd, the retiring directors insisted on having immediate repayment of their loan accounts. S—— M—— were forced to seek additional working capital until they could negotiate the sale and leaseback of B——'s freehold premises. Their clearing bank put up £30,000 against the security of the factory (which was advertised as an investment at £40,000) and the directors were repaid their loans. Unfortunately it took nine months to complete the factory sale, which did not provide sufficient funds to repay the bank. That is the danger in the open-ended bridge.

While the clearing banks are becoming increasingly willing to make longer-term loans for the purchase of plant, the traditional method for smaller sums has been *hire purchase*. This is coming under increasing pressure from *leasing*, which should offer lower monthly payments. But the relative popularity of either is going to depend upon the current tax situation as you read this.

Something that is growing in popularity is *invoice discounting*, where a proportion of the value of an invoice is advanced to the company awaiting payment; this is dealt with later (see pp. 44–5).

Established retailers who make their own hire-purchase agreements with customers may similarly be able to discount these under block arrangements with a finance house.

Sources of Loans   *problems 33–43*

THE CLEARING BANKS

Four-fifths of all loans made possible by the deposits of 13 million personal customers at 12,000 clearing bank branches go to businesses.

There is perhaps little to choose between the 'big four' clearing banks over a period of time when it comes to getting a loan, but on any given day lending policy will differ from bank to bank and branch to branch.

The clearing banks (ignoring subsidiaries) have the following features:

1. The bulk of their loans are overdrafts. They also offer bridging finance, short-term loans and, in a small but growing way, medium-term loans. Long-term loans are almost never made. The argument is that lending long-term is dangerous because bank deposits may be withdrawn either without notice or at short notice. But in reality annually renewed overdraft permissions become longer-term finance anyway and it is in recognition of this that the clearers now encourage more medium-term loans which are repayable in clearly defined stages. This helps the banks avoid the uncertainty of unused overdraft facilities.

2. Money is never intentionally put at risk. To ensure that no risk attaches to loans the banks generally advance no more than 50–65 per cent of the finance required for a project while taking 100 per cent of the project as security. Additional collateral and personal guarantees from company directors may be required (see Chapter One, II), particularly where the bank's share of the financing exceeds 50 per cent. The clearers adopt a conservative approach to valuations, balance sheets etc and cash flows, attaching considerable weight to character and track

record. For this reason it is always essential to build bank confidence by exact fulfilment of obligations.

3. Interest rates at 2 per cent to 5 per cent over bank base (and no profit participation) are said to reflect the low risk nature of loans but they equally reflect the banks' access to cheap funds. Commitment fees are a growing element in bank charges, particularly for bridging loans.

4. The clearers are vulnerable to political pressure on the 'quality' of loans. Thus, from time to time finance for speculative deals will prove difficult.

(See also 'Bank managers', pp. 20–21).

THE MERCHANT BANKS

There are about a hundred merchant banks in the UK, the most exclusive being members of the Accepting Houses Committee, who between them have assets of over £3,000 million. About sixty merchant banks belong to the Issuing Houses Association. ('Accepting' is the guaranteeing of bills of exchange; 'issuing' is the arrangement of share issues.)

1. Merchant banks do not in general give overdrafts; they offer bridging and longer-term finance. Only a part of their funds comes from deposits and it has been the growth of the money market that has allowed them to expand (see below).

2. It is a fallacy that merchant banks commonly offer venture or risk capital. The higher interest rates they charge (up to 5 per cent over finance house base, which is itself often higher than bank base), together with the profit share they inevitably take, reflect not so much the degree of risk as the fact that merchant banks borrow on the money market where funds are expensive. They do not have the same easy ability that the clearers have to borrow directly from the public at low, even nominal, rates of interest. But because of the methods they employ, which clearing banks do not employ, and because those methods generate for them a greater upside gain, they can take on propositions which would not meet clearing bank criteria. They can take a profit share; take actual shares in the borrowing company; put a director on the board of the borrowing company; and charge significant commitment or arrangement fees in addition to interest.

3. The involvement of the merchant bank with a client is clearly greater than the involvement of the clearing bank with a client. Complementary to this is the depth of information the

merchant bank may require according to the circumstances: three, preferably five, years' balance sheets and profit and loss accounts whenever possible; budgets and cash flow projections; biographies of directors and key personnel; meetings with key personnel; product samples; market surveys; factory/site visits; and independent valuations.

4. Merchant banks are not generally interested in lending sums of less than £½ million.

5. Merchant banks have a preference for customers who are growing and with whom the bank can grow and eventually assist towards the new issue market.

THE FRINGE BANKS

Fringe banks were decimated by the property collapse of the early seventies. Today there may or may not be any fringe banks left, depending upon your definition. Fringe banks are perhaps those merchant banks that are not members of either the Accepting Houses Committee or the Issuing Houses Association. They are perhaps simply the post-1960 'merchant banks'. Perhaps they are not even banks at all but merely companies who enter into joint-company arrangements with borrowers and procure money for them from merchant and clearing banks.

THE INSURANCE COMPANIES

The funds handled by the insurance companies are vast. Members of the British Insurance Association have a premium income of one-tenth of the world total. They have sufficient assets to give everyone in Britain about £500 and every hour of every working day they have to place around £½ million.

The only way the smaller businessman can get his hands on any of this money directly (indirectly he might through a loan from one of the merchant banks in whom the insurance companies have stakes) is by an industrial mortgage. The insurance companies will advance a conservative percentage (usually 65 per cent) against a conservative valuation resulting in an ultra-conservative package, not necessarily at a moderate rate of interest.

There is no need to make your approach through a broker.

THE PENSION FUNDS

Strictly for the big boys.

Small investment companies are a useful source of finance for projects resulting in property investment situations. As there is quite a variety of such companies it is often worth advertising propositions.

The approach of such companies can be very flexible and in some respects they have been developing parallel with the insurance companies. During the early years of the last property boom, smart operators were walking all over the insurance and investment people. They would borrow from the insurance company, pension fund, family trust or private investment company to buy and develop a site. They would then sell the completed development to the financiers at a profit – one profit. The backers would then let the building back to the property men – one investment. The property men would sublet – income. So the smart boys took a profit plus income against the financiers' secure but unexciting investment. Now the institutions are becoming more directly involved, taking over the profitable lettings, and the same goes for their smaller distant relations.

EXAMPLES:

(a) G—— L—— Ltd had a factory refurbishment and extension deal. A small family investment company E—— Ltd agreed to provide a 100 per cent loan for G—— L—— Ltd to buy and improve the property on condition that the property would be sold to them at an agreed price after completion and that G—— L—— Ltd would find a suitable tenant in advance.

(b) S—— Manufacturing Ltd had thirty years to run on a 35-year lease. They needed more space and approached the landlords, a family trust, who agreed to advance to them the money to build an extension and the rent was increased accordingly.

THE FINANCE HOUSES

The main business of the finance houses is hire purchase and leasing. Some are independent, some are subsidiaries of the clearing banks and some have themselves become banks. Whether subsidiaries of clearing banks or not the finance houses borrow in the main on the money market which makes them a more expensive source of funds than the clearers.

During the property boom the finance houses moved into development finance on much the same terms as the fringe banks. Some of them subsequently lost very heavily. Nevertheless, property finance is still available from this source, albeit not on the same terms as before.

THE INDUSTRIAL AND COMMERCIAL FINANCE CORPORATION

In 1931 the Macmillan Committee on Finance and Industry reported that there was no source of long-term funds for those companies not large enough to go public. The clearing banks combined to set up ICFC in 1945 to fill this 'Macmillan gap'. Such was the speed of reaction. And only now, approaching fifty years after Macmillan, is ICFC making any attempt to channel funds to the genuinely small business. This is because what Macmillan and ICFC consider a small company and what you and the author consider a small company are totally different things.

To ICFC a company with profits of £10,000 per annum is so small that it hardly exists. And the midget businessman who has been led to expect a sympathetic, generous approach is in for a further shock. ICFC is just as tough as the merchant banks. But where the merchant banks offer speed of decision and the flexible approach of the financial adventurer, ICFC acts with the speed, rigidity and red tape of a senile civil servant.

COMPLEMENTARY COMPANIES

When the professional financiers are not interested (and sometimes even when they are), what better place for the man manufacturing furniture to turn for finance than to a company supplying veneers or itself manufacturing furniture? Such arrangements inevitably result in the company that provides the finance taking a majority stake. But, as they say, half a loaf is better than no bread.

THE INVOICE DISCOUNTERS

There are a number of sources specialising in invoice discounting and factoring, including certain clearing bank subsidiaries. The discounter advances 75–80 per cent against borrowers' sales invoices so that the borrower does not have to wait for money until his customer settles. This improves the cash flow. When the customer does settle, the borrower gets the remaining 25 per cent less the discounter's charges.

A growing trend is for the discounter to take over the client company's entire sales ledger and bad debt protection is generally included. This is called factoring and its viability depends upon average invoice size. The sales ledger service is also available to those who do not wish to discount invoices.

However, the practical drawback to all invoice discounting is that it results in a corresponding loss of borrowing power elsewhere. The book debts are assets of the company and are lost as security for overdrafts and other loans.

THE FINANCE BROKERS

There is nothing the finance broker can do that you cannot do yourself if you try hard enough.

If you do decide to use one never pay any fee or commission in advance of getting a loan.

THE PRIVATE INVESTORS

Every week newspapers, the *Financial Times* in particular, carry advertisements by private individuals looking for investment situations. Sometimes they seek an active role, sometimes not; sometimes a majority shareholding, sometimes not. Terms are entirely by negotiation.

Some merchant banks and financial consultants will also have contacts with private investors.

'VENDOR' FINANCE

When constructing a proposition always look for concessions by vendors etc that will act as a lever with commercial sources.

EXAMPLE: William D—— wanted to buy and develop a building plot at a total cost of £27,000. A local clearing bank agreed to put up £18,000 if D—— would put up £9,000, but D—— had only £5,000 of his own. The vendor agreed to accept half the money for the land at the outset and the remainder out of the proceeds of the sale of the house, and the deal was done with money to spare.

THE MONEY MARKET

The money market exists only between banks, major companies and institutions which borrow and lend money between themselves in blocks of at least £25,000, commonly £1 million, inevitably for less than a week, often overnight. The funds are channelled by money brokers who work on commission.

The business of borrowing money begins a long time before you ever contact a bank. It begins when you start to establish the sort of credentials that will enable you to borrow significant sums of money – that is track record. You enter an active phase as soon as a proposition occurs. You must identify the type of loan and source that the proposition requires before it is finalised so that the requirements of the source may be incorporated (see above). It is foolish to construct a proposition and only then consider the financing problems. You must be aware of these and allow for them at the outset.

The final phase is the presentation to the banker. This should demonstrate:

1. That the proposition meets the financier's criteria, in particular with regard to security; the proportion of bank money to own funds; and repayment.

2. That the proposition is viable.

3. That you have the ability to carry out the proposition.

4. That you can be relied upon to act with integrity, at least as regards the bank.

So you have an appointment with a banker. And that banker has to make his preliminary assessment, at least, sitting in his office. He may not know you at all. It is essential, therefore, that you not only make the right points but that you can produce evidence to back your claims. With you you should have three or five years' balance sheets and profit and loss accounts, where available; cash flow projection; budget; details of securities together with valuations of important assets; written account of the proposition, market surveys etc; samples; and any other evidence, such as photographs, which you can produce to show what you do and how you do it. If you are a sole proprietor you may not be able to produce balance sheets and profit and loss accounts but you should instead have some accounts certified by your accountant or your books or some other evidence of the track record that you are claiming for yourself. (For how to prepare figures see Chapter Three.)

If you have no track record of working for yourself or are starting a new company, then you are immediately at a serious disadvantage, but you are not ruled out. The bank will merely respond by placing you in a higher risk category and consequently by strengthening its protective measures. You must elaborate on every little aspect of your past that has qualified you for this next step – controlling staff, experience of buying materials, negotiating contracts, marketing or whatever it may be. Some of the things may be so obvious to you that they do not seem worth mentioning, but they may not be obvious to the stranger on the other side of the table. It will not pay to be modest. Where material is a little lacking take the molehill you have and make it into a mountain. Where it is seriously lacking you have no choice but to bring in expertise – employees, consultants, co-directors. You must do this, not simply because you will not get the loan otherwise, but because ignorance and inexperience mean failure. Where you have people lined up explain their records to the banker. Bankers believe that they can judge a businessman by the calibre of the people he gathers around him.

The banker steps out of his office to greet you or you are shown into it. This is one of the most important moments in the entire presentation. You will be weighing up the banker and he will be weighing you up. 'Is this the sort of man', he will ask himself, 'to whom I can lend money? Is he reliable? Has he got what it takes? Has he got success written all over him or do I detect the odour of a loser?' The human animal is a perceptive animal, and the banker is trained to judge character. He will notice how you dress and how you sit and how you twitch.

Early on you must make an impact. In the way you speak and in what you say you must demonstrate not only that you have the paper qualifications but also that you have the character to withstand and overcome the considerable problems that beset all small businessmen.

If the banker begins by asking you trivial questions your heart sinks. If he asks you for your full name and age and the address of your last bank etc, then, unless this is a small routine loan or you know that the application is gilt-edged, you have trouble. You are dealing with a man who probably lacks experience and who is clinging to the book, to the rules. You have a proposition, a reasonable proposition, but like most it has some flaws and unless you can get him away from his little book of rules you've had it.

You must assert yourself. You must sweep aside the (rather insulting) trivia and bring him on to the plusses: look Mr Bank Manager, *this* is my proposition, *this* is what is good about it, and kindly don't waste my time with this nonsense. I'm doing

47

you a favour coming here. Either treat me properly or I'll go somewhere else.

Every banker has his own standard questions. 'Why have you brought this to me?' is an obvious one. He wants to know who else you have asked. The fact that another bank has turned you down is probably best avoided, but each banker will make his own decision, and sometimes one will take pleasure in the fact that he has the judgement to back you when others have refused. He is bound to ask questions about the preparation of the figures. 'Why do you expect to spend £x in April but £y in May?' 'What is the size of the market for this product?' 'What would be the effect of a 10 per cent wage increase?' You must have answers. Almost any answer is better than no answer.

Check all figure work meticulously. An error would be fatal. There is the old story about the director of a Slater Walker subsidiary who approached the 'great man' with a scheme he had been working on for several weeks. Slater picked up the projections, immediately spotted an error, tore the papers up and then completely ignored the man. (Ironically, Slater has now had to learn what it is like to have figures torn up.) So you also had your figures torn up? You didn't get the loan? Don't let it worry you. That presentation was just a rehearsal; every failure is a rehearsal, is experience. Now you know the weak spots in your presentation, go away, rework it, and try again somewhere else. Keep notes on every source you approach; another time you may have a proposition that suits them.

PROBLEMS AND SOLUTIONS

22. I am being pressed to settle a debt but am short of funds. Can I send a post-dated cheque?
You can, provided you are certain you can meet the cheque on the due date; it will undoubtedly keep your creditor quiet if it is not dated too far ahead. But bear in mind that if the cheque ultimately bounces it will assist your creditors to obtain a quick judgement against you.

23. Due to a slump in sales I no longer need and cannot afford to pay for goods which were delivered a month ago.

If by their nature the goods are readily saleable you should contact your supplier, explain the situation and ask him to accept the goods back. As you will be in breach of contract he will be entitled to sue for damages and this will probably be the difference between the price you were to pay for the goods and the price your supplier actually obtains elsewhere, plus costs. With goods that are easily saleable, damages can only be small and therefore if your supplier refuses to co-operate return the goods anyway. But if the goods are, for example, packaging bearing your brand name the goods would be unsaleable elsewhere, damages would possibly exceed the cost of the goods and it would be pointless returning them. In this case you can only negotiate for time to pay.

You always have the right to reject goods when there is a significant departure from the terms of the contract for them.

24. This morning I received a writ for £2,500. When does the crunch come?

If you have a defence you must normally enter an appearance within fourteen days, but your solicitor should be able to get this time doubled. A High Court case can take two years or more, and as this is a writ for more than £2,000, a High Court case is what it will be. You and your creditor swear affidavits which are considered by a Master. The Master allows two to five minutes per case. If you have made a reasonable defence he will send the case for trial, and it is the waiting for that trial that may take two years.

If you believe the Master will rule against you a request for an adjournment should be good for two weeks. If he does find against you an appeal is good for a month.

If you simply have a cash flow problem, consider producing a cash flow diagram to your bank and asking for assistance. Consider what you can do to improve liquidity and consider negotiating for time to pay.

25. My company has been served with a notice under Section 223 of the Companies Act 1948 requiring payment within three weeks, failing which the creditor will petition for compulsory winding-up.

A company that fails to pay within three weeks of receiving such a notice demonstrates inability to meet its debts, one of the conditions under which a company may be compulsorily wound up. To avoid this you must either settle or satisfy the court that you have a reasonable defence to the claim, in which case the petitioners will first have to sue to prove the debt and only then petition for a winding-up. A company may not be wound up on a petition by a creditor or group of creditors for less than £200.

26. A customer has owed money for three months. Only after I issued a writ did he complain that the goods were faulty and he has now replied to the writ to this effect.

A customer should always return or promptly reject faulty goods and the fact that this was not done is in your favour. You may, indeed, decide to ask for the goods back, particularly if, by their nature, you are able to resell them without loss. If it transpires that the debtor has converted or resold them his defence all but collapses, unless the goods are of such a type that the fault would not have been immediately apparent. The return of perfect goods does not prevent your claiming for the difference between the price charged to the customer and the price eventually obtained elsewhere.

When it comes to the hearing you must anticipate that the debtor will fabricate evidence and be ready for this. If it is a High Court action, where the only chance of a quick judgement is before a Master, it would be fatal to go into this preliminary hearing without as complete an answer as possible, as otherwise the case may be sent for trial and you can say goodbye to your money for up to two years. (See Chapter Five on contract.)

27. The threat of a writ used to scare debtor companies into payment. Now it may be so long before cases are heard that writs have lost their impact.

An alternative scare tactic in the case of companies is to serve a notice under Section 223 of the Companies Act 1948 on the registered office of the debtor requiring payment within three weeks. If payment is not made you may petition for winding-up. A scare tactic in the case of partnerships may be to sue one partner rather than all partners jointly. The partner sued, fearing difficulty in obtaining equalising sums from his fellow partners, may then pressure them into settling with you promptly.

28. My company manufactures toys. To cope with Christmas demand we are obliged to manufacture steadily throughout the year and stockpile. This is a heavy financial burden.

You may be able to improve the position to a degree by attending to the matters already raised in this chapter, but in an industry with an innate cash flow problem the only solution is to introduce lines that have a different season. Thus, beach toys and accessories could fit in well. If you lack resources consider a merger (see Chapter Four).

29. In my business I need to stock 300 different types of component. During the annual stock-take I discovered up to two years' supply of some and only two weeks' of others.

If it takes an annual stock-take to reveal this then there is a serious problem with management technique (see Chapter Three). You should have a physical count at least twice a year. In addition, you must have a control system that will enable you to record every addition to and removal from stock. This is also important for accounting purposes. For a complex range of stock, consider a micro-computer.

30. How can I buy a tax loss company to reduce tax liability?

Such companies are occasionally advertised in the financial press or your accountant may be able to put you on to one. You do need a good accountant because there are various restrictions; the device will not succeed where, for example, the company has ceased to trade. You may also have to purchase the debts of the company from banks etc.

31. What can I do to reduce my company's liability to tax on a capital gain following a sale and leaseback?

As you are not buying another factory you lose the ability to postpone the tax under roll-over provisions. But the tax may still be postponed if you use the proceeds of the sale to purchase certain other classes of assets. These are fixed plant and machinery; ships; aircraft; hovercraft; and goodwill.

A capital gain can be offset against a trading loss for the same or the preceding accounting period.

32. My company owns a freehold factory valued at £100,000

on which the bank have a charge for their lending of from
£10,000 to £40,000, depending on the time of year. Profits are
running at £12,000 on a turnover of £180,000. We could
improve the former by cutting borrowing and the latter by
more investment; would sale and leaseback be a good idea?
See the advantages and disadvantages under 'Sale and leaseback', p. 34. On these figures it looks best to sell the business,
keep the freehold and let it out.

**33. Each year I have to renegotiate a company overdraft. This
is a big worry.**
A clearing bank may agree to convert to a medium-term loan,
particularly where the overdraft is being used in part to finance
equipment. You may need more permanent capital; see
'Sources of Loans', pp. 40–6.

**34. I am a clothing wholesaler and have the opportunity to
buy a huge parcel of dresses from a company in liquidation at
a knock-down price. I need £15,000 urgently.**
This is precisely the self-liquidating overdraft situation the
clearers like.
**34a. The clearing bank turned me down on the grounds that
the fashion business is very risky.**
You have to convince the bank firstly that the dresses are saleable, and secondly of a date by which the bank will be taken
out. Convert an open situation to something, in part, back-to-
back, by taking orders against samples borrowed from the
receiver.

**35. I have a deal set up to purchase a chain of six retail outlets.
Even allowing that I sell the freeholds and lease back I still
have financing problems.**
It may be that an investment company will assist you with additional finance for the chance of obtaining the six freehold
investments.

**36. My bank manager agreed to back me on a proposition
provided I obtained certain terms. I duly negotiated the deal
along the agreed lines but then he reneged.**
It is unlikely that you will have any legal redress (see Chapter

Five on contract), but take this up with the bank's area office. While banks like people to think that they only act with the utmost integrity they are, after all, only staffed by human beings having the same weaknesses that we all have.

37. I want to manufacture my invention. The only source of finance I have been able to interest wants 60 per cent of the profits.

Presumably this is to be a joint company arrangement with a 60:40 share split. Assuming that you really have exhausted all possibilities (have you tried the National Research Development Corporation?) consider that 40 per cent of something is better than all of nothing; that there will always be another invention which you will be able to finance on better terms if this one is successful; and that perhaps you would be wise to license manufacturers to produce your product, collect royalties and think of other inventions and not get involved in the production at all.

38. In a joint company deal where I hold only 49 per cent of the shares I am being asked to guarantee 100 per cent of any losses.

This is not only unfair, it is also dangerous. While you remain good for the guarantee it is your money that is actually at risk but you have no control. Resist the terms.

39. I have agreed terms subject to contract for the purchase of six building plots and the price is very low. Even so I still find myself unable to raise the finance to buy and develop.

Consider asking for a six-month completion with a low deposit. Then you have time either to find the money to complete the purchase or to sell on at a profit. Consider asking the vendor to leave half his money in the project, which would make financing easier. Consider introducing the land to another party and taking a commission.

40. I thought I had the answer to my problems when I discovered invoice discounting but now I see that the general charge given to my bank precludes this.

Your bank is treating your book debts as part of the security for your overdraft and therefore if you wish to discount invoices you will need their permission, in which case they will doubtless reduce your overdraft limit. However, as discounters generally advance 80 per cent against invoices whereas banks tend to value at 60–70 per cent it is possible that you will see some marginal increase in finance available overall. Against this, discounting has the disadvantage that funds can only be available after goods have been sold and not during the manufacturing process.

41. I paid a fee of 1 per cent (£1,000) to a broker but the loan never materialised.
Your remedy depends upon the circumstances in which the money was paid (see Chapter Five on contract).

42. I recently obtained planning permission to demolish my home and erect six new units. My bank manager has turned down my request for building finance on the grounds that I have no experience.
Bring in some experience. Alternatively, if you think you know better than your bank manager, sell sufficient plots to finance the building of one unit – and you will have your experience.

43. My request for a facility of £10,000 has been refused by area office although it had the support of my bank manager.
Ask for a meeting with area office. They try to keep away from customers but they may agree to see you. Otherwise, try another bank, preferably one where the manager can go to £10,000 on his own authority.

USEFUL BOOKS

Bond, George Dennis, *Corporate Finance for Management* (Butterworth, 1974)

Firth, Michael, *Management of Working Capital* (Macmillan, 1976)

Forman, Martin, and John Gilbert, *Factoring and Finance* (Heinemann, 1976)

Merrett, A.J., and Allen Sykes, *Capital Budgeting and Company Finance* (Longman, 1973)

3
FIGURES

In which we consider how to prepare figures for presentation
to a bank or for corporation tax and how to interpret figures
presented to you; the profit and loss account; the balance
sheet; the budget; the cash flow; and management accounts.

When Robert Maxwell's Pergamon Press was to be taken over
by Leasco Data Processing Equipment Corporation, an independent investigation by accountants Price Waterhouse revealed a loss of £495,000 in 1968 compared with a profit
reported to shareholders of £2.1 million. And in the first six
months of 1969 there was a loss of nearly £2 million compared
to Maxwell's forecast for the year of a £2.5 million profit.

Said Maxwell: 'Accounting is not the exact science which
some of us once thought it was.'

I THE PROFIT AND LOSS ACCOUNT

As regards small private companies the profit and loss account
fulfils three functions: it can be produced to a bank in support of
a loan application; a copy has to be filed at Companies House
for the benefit of creditors etc; and it is the basis for the assessment of corporation tax.

There is an obvious conflict between the first and last of these
functions. One way of overcoming this is to present unaudited
accounts to your bank if they will accept them, where you
intend that the audited accounts should take a pessimistic view
for tax purposes. One thing is certain: if you reduce your liability to corporation tax you will not need the same bank facility
as otherwise.

On the other hand, where profit in real terms is genuinely
low, the present legislation on stock relief has substantially removed the tax penalty on bumping stock values to produce an

illusory increase in profit. This should be kept in mind when interpreting accounts.

The profit and loss account can be manipulated in either direction by the following devices:

1. Stock valuation.
2. Depreciation.
3. Extraordinary expenses and receipts.

EXAMPLES:

(a) Company X starts a financial period with £10,000 worth of stocks, makes purchases worth £15,000 during the period and has a turnover of £40,000. What is the gross profit?

Turnover	£40,000
Opening stock	£10,000
Purchases	£15,000
Profit	?

You say £15,000? You say £25,000? You can say any figure you like, because something is missing without which all the other figures are meaningless. This is closing stock. Insert a figure of £10,000 closing stock into the above and you have a profit of £25,000. Insert £15,000 and you have a profit of £30,000.

Yet the Companies Acts allow that an auditor does not have to make an independent valuation of stocks nor even supervise counting. He is merely obliged to ask for a signed statement from an officer of the company giving his valuation, the normal basis of which is the lower of current value or cost (see pp. 33–4, on taxation).

If the officer undervalues no one will criticise; it is only prudent to take a cautious view. Of course, liability for corporation tax will be reduced – but the officer won't have been thinking of that, will he?

(b) Company X will have to put a value on plant as well as trading stocks. Machinery depreciates in value each year and the auditor normally uses a rigid formula for calculating how much to deduct from profits to take account of this, either on a 'straight line' basis or on a 'reducing balance' basis.

Under the straight line method a fixed sum of money is deducted each year. If a machine cost £1,200 and is expected to last ten years, then £120 is deducted each year. Under the reducing balance method a fixed percentage of the residual value is deducted each year. Thus, the same machine might be depreciated by 25 per cent of its £1,200 cost in the first year (£300) and by 25 per cent of the reduced balance of £900 in the second year, and so on. The latter method gives more dramatic depreciation and thus lower profits in the early years, with higher profits later, and the reverse applies to the first method.

But there is not only a choice of method; there is also the question of the number of years over which a machine is to be depreciated. To complicate matters further it is possible that while a machine is being depreciated its true value is actually rising (in money terms) due to inflation.

The same sort of considerations apply to research and development costs.

(c) Company X has made a massive capital gain on the sale of part of its yard to a property company. Company Y has closed down a factory and as a result made very substantial redundancy payments. If these unusual, once-only items are incorporated into the profit and loss account without explanation and are not treated separately, they give a misleading impression of the underlying trends. But they could be so included.

Table B

One Company: One Year — Three Profit and Loss Accounts

£000s	1		2		3	
1. Turnover		100		100		100
2. Opening stock	20		20		20	
3. Purchases	30		30		27	
4. Wages	30		30		27	
	80		80		74	
5. *Less:* closing stock	20		25		30	
	60		55		44	
6. Gross margin		40		45		56
7. Overheads	35		30		36	
8. Depreciation	10		4		2	
9. Research and development	6		2		1	
	51		36		39	
10. Net profit		-11		+9		+17
11. Extraordinary expenses				5		5
		-11		+4		+12

57

Table B shows three profit and loss accounts prepared for the same company and for the same accounting period.

In profit and loss account 1 the directors have taken a pessimistic view. They have just taken over the company and want to get all the skeletons out of the cupboard so that the following year they can show how their skill has turned the company round. (Their skill lies in the manipulation of figures.)

In profit and loss account 2 the directors have taken a neutral view; they feel that it gives, in the words of Section 149 of the Companies Act 1948, 'a true and fair view of the company's profit or loss'.

In profit and loss account 3 the directors have presented the figures in the most optimistic way. They wish to sell the company.

False Statements

Section 19 of the Companies Act 1976 states that it is an offence punishable by up to two years' imprisonment or a fine or both for an officer of a company to make a false statement, either orally or in writing, to an auditor either recklessly or knowingly. But where will the judiciary draw the line between misleading statements and those that are either cautious or, alternatively, somewhat optimistic?

It is unlikely that the directors have done anything illegal in their preparation of accounts 1, 2 or 3.

1. Turnover is at the same figure in all three versions.

2. The opening stock figure must remain the same in all versions; it is the previous year's closing stock figure.

3. Purchases. This heading embraces the raw materials of manufacturers or the trading stocks of retailers or wholesalers and should not include purchases made in connection with the management of the company, such as writing paper etc. There are always grey areas, and these enable the directors preparing version 3 to take £3,000 out of purchases and insert it under overheads. For why, see item 6.

4. Wages. This heading embraces the wages paid to the factory workers, the warehousemen or the shop staff. Salaries paid to management are entered as overheads. Again there are grey areas enabling the removal of £3,000 from wages in version 3 and its insertion under overheads. For why, see item 6.

5. Closing stock. The value of stock is rarely a simple matter of fact. Problem areas are slow-moving lines – should they be

valued at cost or less than cost?; damaged goods; work-in-progress; and manufactured goods.

6. Gross margin is a key indicator. It is the margin of profit that is made on prime costs (usually labour and materials). Where gross margin is low for the type of business or is declining, the analyst, perhaps a banker, may infer that there is something fundamentally wrong, something that it may not be possible to correct – a bad product from either the production or marketing point of view. In version 1 gross margin is 40 per cent of turnover after a pessimistic stock valuation; in version 2 gross margin is 45 per cent of turnover after a neutral stock valuation; in version 3 gross margin is a massive 56 per cent of turnover following an optimistic stock valuation and the manipulation of purchases and wages.

7. Overheads. Under the Companies Acts details of overheads are not required, but in a full profit and loss account the figure for overheads would be broken down into different categories – lighting and heating, rent and rates, postage, salaries, professional fees etc. In preparing version 1 the directors have included an extraordinary expense of £5,000; in version 2 this is dealt with separately (see item 11); and in version 3 it is again dealt with separately but the figure has been inflated by the addition of transfers from purchases and wages.

8. Depreciation has been calculated on the same figure of £20,000 in each version but different methods have been employed. In version 1 the auditor has agreed to the reducing balance method depreciating by 50 per cent per annum. In version 2 depreciation is by straight line based on a life of five years and in version 3 on a life of ten years.

9. Research and development costs have been based on the same figure of £6,000 in each example. In preparing version 1 the directors have decided to write off the entire cost in the first year. In version 2 the reducing balance approach has been employed at a rate of 33⅓ per cent. Version 3 is based on an optimistic six years' life expectancy and the cost is written down by the straight line method.

10. The directors who have just taken over show a loss (by their predecessors) of £11,000; the directors who have no axe to grind show a profit of £9,000; the directors who wish to sell out show a massive £17,000 profit.

11. In versions 2 and 3 the directors now have to make provision for the extraordinary expense that the directors, in

preparing version 1, decided to incorporate into their ordinary trading results. Final results now range from a £12,000 profit to an £11,000 loss.

Table C

Profit and Loss Accounts for Three Consecutive Years

£000s	Year 1		Year 2		Year 3	
1. Turnover		100		105		121
2. Opening stock	20		25		32	
3. Purchases	30		33		24	
4. Wages	30		35		35	
	80		93		91	
5. *Less:* closing stock	25		32		25	
	55		61		66	
6. Gross margin		45		44		55
7. Overheads	30		34.7		36	
8. Depreciation	4		4		4	
9. Research and development	2		1.3		2	
	36		40		42	
10. Net profit		9		4		13
11. Extraordinary expense		5				
		4				

Table C above shows three profit and loss accounts prepared for the same manufacturing company for three consecutive years, taking the 'neutral' column 2 from Table B as year 1.

From an examination of three or five consecutive accounts the analyst can form an opinion as to their accuracy and at the same time infer a great deal about the health, management and prospects of a company.

1. Turnover. Assuming steady inflation of 10 per cent per annum there was an actual decline in sales volume between years 1 and 2 and a 5 per cent increase between years 2 and 3. Over the three-year period there was no real growth.

2. Opening stock is the previous year's closing stock.

3. Purchases. A dramatic fall in purchases in year 3 requires investigation. The implications are: less wastage of raw materials; cheaper materials; increased mark-up; or stock reduction. The latter would appear to be confirmed by item 5.

4. Wages. The apparently disproportionate increase in the wage bill in year 2 implies either low productivity or a big wage rise. But it might be that the goods manufactured did not contribute to turnover and confirmation of this lies in the high closing stock figure for year 2. In year 3 the wage bill remains at the year 2 level implying greater productivity; no wage rise; the sale of products requiring less processing; or reduction in stock level for manufactures. The fall in purchases appears to rule out the third implication, while the reduced closing stock level for the year appears to confirm the fourth.

5. Closing stock. A disproportionate increase in closing stock or consistent excess stock is always a danger sign. The increase in year 2 over year 1 of approaching one-third implies slow-moving or redundant stock; sales below expectations; poor stock control; or an 'optimistic' stock valuation.

6. Gross margin is 45 per cent of turnover in year 1, falls to around 42 per cent in year 2 and then recovers to 45 per cent in year 3. A gross margin which is low for the industry or which is declining when expressed as a percentage of turnover implies bad costing; low productivity – either in use of labour or materials; or a bad product.

7. Overheads. A full account with a breakdown of overheads would be required to reveal the cause of the disproportionate increase in year 2.

10. Net profit should be expressed as a percentage of turnover and a comparison made with previous years and with other companies in the same industry. The analyst will also make the same comparisons with net profit expressed as a percentage of capital employed, for which figure he will have to turn to the balance sheet.

II THE BALANCE SHEET

The balance sheet is a more significant document than the profit and loss account. It is divided into two parts; the first shows how the capital employed in the business has been used, the second where it came from. By definition the two sides must balance.

Albeit the balance sheet is such an important document for the analyst it has two flaws:

1. It shows the assets and liabilities of a company on one specific date only. This will always be the last day of the

accounting period for which the profit and loss account has been prepared. For that one day the situation of a company may be contrived to look rather different from the way it would look on any of the other 364 days of the year.

EXAMPLE: Before the exempt private company was abolished, the director/shareholders could make themselves loans from the company funds. By drawing loans instead of salaries they avoided tax. Today a loan may not be made to a director except in special circumstances. But what if the loan is repaid two or three weeks before the balance sheet date and redrawn shortly after? The balance sheet will reveal no clue to the Revenue because the loan, an asset of the company, will not exist at the balance sheet date.

2. The valuation of assets, on which the balance sheet is based, may be inaccurate. Therefore, every banker examining a balance sheet for asset cover for an intended loan has his own formula for compensating for this inaccuracy and for the write-down necessary in a winding-up. Basically, only half the value shown is attributed to stock and about two-thirds the value of debtors. If a banker has special knowledge which inclines him to reduce these figures further, then he will do so.

Clearly, what you, as a businessman, consider adequate asset cover for a loan and what a banker considers adequate are going to be two different things.

Table D is a simplified version of the capital employment part of a balance sheet. It shows, in column one, what capital has been spent on, and what is owed to and by the company. In the second column is given a banker's interpretation of those figures.

1. Fixed assets are those items which do not form part of the company's trading stock; are not intended for sale; or could not be sold quickly. Examples are buildings, machinery, furniture etc.

2. Plant. The figure shown is the value attached to plant at the end of the previous year.

3. Additions. Expenditure on plant during the current year.

4. Depreciation. Valuation of plant for balance sheet purposes is normally by depreciation in accordance with a predetermined scale and despite inflation it is rare for plant to be revalued. (The depreciation figure shown in a balance sheet is not necessarily that allowable for tax purposes.) As a rule of thumb a banker will value at half the depreciated figure.

Table D

One Balance Sheet — Two Versions

£000s			The banker's interpretation	
1. *Fixed assets*				
2. Plant	25			
3. Additions	10			
4. Depreciation	7			
	28		14	
5. Property	50		46	
6. Total		78		60
7. *Current assets*				
8. Debtors	45		30	
9. Stock	40		20	
10. Prepayments	3		3	
	88		53	
11. *Current liabilities*				
12. Trade creditors	30			
13. Other creditors	10			
14. Overdraft	25			
	65		65	
15. Net current assets		23		(-12)
16. Total		101		48

5. Property. The value of freehold or leasehold premises occupied by the company would come under this heading. But the land bank of a building company would be more likely to be shown under current assets. Bankers like property and in this example a write-down of only £4,000 to cope with a forced sale has been allowed.

6. Total (net fixed assets). The banker has allowed a total value for fixed assets of £60,000 as against a balance sheet figure of £78,000.

7. Current assets are cash; trading stock; assets intended for sale; and assets that could be realised quickly – an investment in public company shares. In reality it may take longer to dispose of items described as current assets than it would items included under fixed assets.

8. Debtors are customers who owe money. Bankers find that when a company is in liquidation debtors do not pay readily, preferring to keep their funds for new suppliers. In this case the banker has put a value of only £30,000 against the £45,000 shown by the balance sheet.

9. Stock. This will be the same figure that is shown as closing stock in the profit and loss account. An auditor is not obliged to stock-take himself; he can accept a certificate stating the amount and value of stock signed by an officer of the company (see p. 34). Bankers are naturally wary of trading stocks and will possibly want to know how and by whom they were valued. Their difficulties are disposing *en bloc* of the stocks of a company in liquidation and the 'disappearance' of stocks immediately prior to a liquidation. As a consequence most types of stock are valued at only 50 per cent. Property is a notable exception because it holds its value and it cannot 'disappear'.

An attempt to forestall a banker's pessimism by overvaluing will be penalised by an increase in corporation tax.

10. Prepayments occur with rent, which is normally paid in advance, or where a company pays for goods before it receives them.

11. Current liabilities are those which will or might have to be met in the short term.

12. Trade creditors are those to whom money is owed by way of trade.

13. Other creditors might be Customs and Excise, landlords, local authorities, employees due holiday pay etc.

14. Overdraft. As an overdraft is repayable on demand it is a current liability. On the other hand, an auditor might show a long-term loan on the capital employed side of the balance sheet.

15. Net current assets. After adjusting current assets downwards, the banker considers that they are exceeded by current liabilities by £12,000. According to the balance sheet, current assets exceed current liabilities by £23,000.

16. By combining items 6 and 15 above the banker concludes that there is a total of fixed and net current assets of only £48,000. The balance sheet shows £101,000. So where did the money come from? This is shown by the other half of the balance sheet, the capital employed side (Table E).

17. Share capital. The more substantial the figure the happier the banker. Shareholders' capital can only be repaid with

Capital Employed

£000s

17. Share capital	25
18. Reserves	50
19. Profit and loss account	10
20. Directors' loan accounts	16
21. Total	101

court permission (see Problem 7) or on a winding-up, where shareholders rank behind all other creditors.

18. Reserves are the profits retained in previous years.

19. Profit and loss account. This is the profit transferred from the profit and loss account – that is, the profit made in the accounting period up to the date of the balance sheet.

20. Directors' loan accounts generally arise where directors vote salaries which go beyond the company's ability to pay and part of the salary is therefore loaned back. Where the director pays tax at a lower rate than the company, such a manoeuvre may also be for tax avoidance.

21. Total capital employed must by definition equal the total of fixed and net current assets shown in the capital employment part of the balance sheet. It does, at £101,000.

(If the balance sheet is presented with liabilities on one side and assets on the other, then on the liabilities side will be share capital, reserves, current liabilities etc., and on the assets side fixed assets, investments, current assets etc.)

Further Analysis

ASSET COVER FOR A LOAN

The banker looks firstly on an unsecured basis. He examines the ratio of fixed and current assets to current liabilities, long-term loans and share capital; examines the same ratio after the loan application has been injected; and looks to see what can be done to strengthen the bank's position on an unsecured basis, albeit he intends to create either a specific or general charge. Only then does he look on a secured basis.

EXAMPLE: Company X produces the balance sheet shown in Tables D and E in support of a loan application of £35,000 for new plant. There are fixed assets of £60,000 and current assets of £53,000 to meet current liabilities plus directors' loan accounts plus shareholders' claims. That is £113,000 to meet claims of £106,000 – only just enough. Inject a new liability of £35,000 and the company becomes insolvent. Allow £18,000 for the realisable value of the plant and the company is solvent again, but only just. Even on an unsecured basis shareholders rank behind the bank and if the directors will agree to convert their loan accounts to shares, effectively preventing them re-paying themselves, then the position improves to 113:65. Now inject the £35,000 loan, allowing £18,000 to be added to assets, and the ratio becomes 131:100.

The loan is approved. The banker has only to protect himself against future losses, fraud etc, and this he can do with a first charge on the property if available, or a second charge if not, and a general charge. The precise terms must be by negotiation.

LIQUIDITY
The banker can assess liquidity by either the debtor:creditor ratio or the current asset:current liability ratio.

EXAMPLE: The company in Table D owes £40,000 to trade and other creditors but is itself owed only £45,000. There are bound to be slow payers and even bad debts and therefore the company's liquidity must come under pressure. Either it delays settling its own accounts or the overdraft goes up.

Looking at the overall current asset:current liability ratio the balance sheet reveals 88:65. Clearing banks consider anything less than 2:1 as unhealthy, unless there are special considerations.

Occasionally a balance sheet may be manipulated to give a different impression or a company may take action to produce a healthier ratio.

EXAMPLES:
(a) If the company in Table D has opened negotiations for sale and leaseback, the auditor might agree to insert the property into current assets. If the banker allows £46,000 for the property the current asset:current liability ratio then becomes 134:65.

(b) If the company in Table D converts the overdraft into a

long-term loan then it disappears across to the other side of the balance sheet (into Table E). The capital employed figure would then go up to £126,000, the current liability figure would be reduced, the net current asset figure and therefore total capital employment figure would increase by £25,000 and the sheet would still balance. Magic. The current asset:current liability ratio would improve to 88:40.

OTHER RATIOS
Debtors:turnover
The debtor figure in Table D is £45,000. Assuming an annual turnover of £270,000 the implication is that an average of two months' credit is taken by customers. From an annual turnover of £135,000 four months' credit may be inferred, but there is a danger in averages. With a seasonal trade then on an annual turnover of £135,000, £30,000 worth may be done in each of the three months up to Christmas. Thus, a debtor figure of £45,000 on 31 December gives a bad impression but might in fact represent only six weeks' credit. Thus, choice of audit date can be important.

Trade creditors:purchases
The figure for trade creditors in Table D is £30,000. Assuming purchases for the year of £120,000 then the ratio between the two is 1:4, indicating that the company is enjoying an average three months' credit from suppliers. The remarks above on averages apply here equally.

The ratios above are significant to a banker; he likes to see a company allowing minimum credit while at the same time taking maximum credit.

Company funds:borrowed funds
Company funds in Table E are share capital, reserves and profits for the current year amounting to £85,000. Banks like to see a ratio here of 2:1 and this is observed with borrowed money amounting to £41,000 (overdraft £25,000, directors' loans £16,000). But banks will discard the 2:1 ratio where security is available outside the company or where the nature of the security inside the company is very solid. Thus, during the property boom of the early seventies banks allowed their customers to become very highly geared, sometimes lending

hundreds of thousands to companies with share capitals of £100. Conservative bankers today point to the fringe bank collapse as evidence that traditional ratios should not be abandoned again.

III THE BUDGET

The budget is a document similar to the profit and loss account, but whereas the latter should be a factual record of past income and expenditure, the budget is a projection for the future.

For an existing business that projection will normally be made from the previous year's results, but in the case of a new project there will have to be market research to arrive at a turnover figure and detailed costing exercises to arrive at expenditure.

There are always two sorts of budget: the one that the businessman prepares for his own use and the one that he prepares for his bank.

Mr X is managing director of the company whose profit and loss account is reproduced in full in Table F in column 1. (A shortened version of this account has already been given in Tables B and C.) Column 2 shows the budget forecast that Mr X has prepared for his own use for the following year. Mr X needs to renew his overdraft facility. In support of his application he produces the manipulated projection shown in column 3.

1. Turnover was £100,000. Mr X believes he can do no better than maintain sales volume, producing a turnover of £110,000 at current prices. This will not satisfy the bank; Mr X budgets for £125,000 turnover in the version prepared for them.

2. Opening stock was £20,000. As one year's closing stock is the next year's opening stock the figure in both projections must be £25,000, the closing stock figure from the profit and loss account.

3. Purchases were £30,000. Mr X expects to maintain this figure by reducing stock levels (by volume, if not value) and also inserts this figure into his manipulated projection against the higher turnover of £125,000.

4. Wages were running at £30,000. Knowing the negotiated wage increase Mr X forecasts £35,000 and maintains this figure for the bank, even against the increased turnover. His explanation is higher productivity.

The Profit and Loss Account, Budget Projection and
Budget Manipulation

£000s	1	2	3
1. Turnover	100	110	125
2. Opening stock	20	25	25
3. Purchases	30	30	30
4. Wages	30	35	35
5. *Less:* closing stock	25	25	22
	55	65	68
6. Gross margin	45	45	57
7. Rent and rates	5	6	5.5
8. Insurance	1	1.5	1.5
9. Light and heat	0.5	0.7	0.6
10. Telephone	0.5	0.75	0.75
11. Stationery and postage	0.5	0.75	0.75
12. Salaries	10	10	11
13. Motoring and van expenses	3	4	3.75
14. Commission	3	3.5	4.5
15. Travel	1	1.5	1.25
16. Sundry	1	1.5	1.25
17. Professional fees	0.5	0.7	0.5
18. Audit	0.5	0.75	0.6
19. Bad debts	0.5	0.6	0.4
20. Depreciation	4	4.5	4.5
21. Research and development	2	1.5	1.33
22. Interest charges	3	3	3
23. Net profit	9	3.75	15.82
24. Extraordinary expense	5	—	—
	4	3.75	15.82

5. Closing stock. Mr X believes he will finish the new year
with much the same value of stock as in the previous year. But
to the bank he gives the dramatically low figure of £22,000, enabling him to produce a very positive cash flow projection (see
Part IV of this chapter).

6. Gross margin, as revealed by the accounts, was a healthy
45 per cent. Mr X expects this to decline to 41 per cent, a figure
that it would be fatal for him to present to his bank. By manipulating his prime costs he has produced a gross margin of
£57,000 on sales of £125,000, which is 45.6 per cent. The bank
will be happy.

7. Rent and rates were £5,000. Mr X knows that the rateable value of his factory has been increased, involving payment of an additional £1,000. His bank manager does not know; for him Mr X shows an increase of only £500.

8. Insurance. Mr X already knows that there will be an increase of the order of 50 per cent, a figure that still looks realistic on turnover of £125,000.

9. Light and heat. A 40 per cent increase is on the cards but as approximately the same amount will be consumed in producing £125,000 as £100,000, the bank will not query 20 per cent.

10. Telephone. In doing more business Mr X must do more telephoning. A 50 per cent increase looks realistic for both projections.

11. Stationery and postage. As item 10.

12. Salaries paid to office staff and directors were £10,000. Although office staff must have an increase Mr X intends to absorb this by taking a cut himself. But for the benefit of the bank he shows the increase they would expect to see.

13. Motoring and van expenses were £3,000. Mr X expects an increase of £1,000 but cuts this to £750 for the benefit of the bank.

14. Commission. Mr X sells some goods through commission agents. In reality he expects an increase from £3,000 to £3,500 but shows £4,500 to the bank, an increase that would be necessary for turnover to reach £125,000.

15. Travel. Mr X allows for an extra £500, but for the bank a lesser increase of £250 will still look realistic.

16. Sundry. As item 15.

17. Professional fees are mainly those of debt collectors. Mr X expects to have to use their services even more in the future, but tells the bank that his new credit control system will actually reduce the number of slow payers.

18. Audit. Mr X has been told by his auditor to expect a bill of £750 but estimates £600 for the benefit of the bank.

19. Bad debts are bound to increase, but the 'new credit control system' will take care of that!

20. Depreciation was running at £4,000. Mr X intends buying more plant and therefore the figure must increase. Mr X will use his investment to explain the higher productivity his bank-version budget claims.

21. Research and development cost the previous year were £6,000, of which £2,000 was written off in the profit and loss

account – a reducing balance scale of 33⅓ per cent. This will mean allowing for one-third of the reduced balance of £4,000 in the budget, plus a further £170 against current expenditure. For the bank Mr X ignores current expenditure.

22. Interest charges were £3,000 and Mr X expects them to remain at the same level. In his manipulated budget he maintains the £3,000 as in his cash flow he intends to show the same facility requirement for £125,000 as in reality he will need for £110,000 turnover.

23. Net profit was £9,000 – only £4,000 after deducting that extraordinary expense (item 24). This year Mr X expects only £3,750 profit, amounting to only 3.4 per cent of turnover as against 4 per cent previously and 9 per cent before the extraordinary expense. But by various manipulations Mr X has produced a healthy 12.5 per cent profit in his forecast to the bank.

IV THE CASH FLOW FORECAST

Money is continually flowing into and out of a business as customers pay for goods or services supplied and creditors' accounts are settled. When a company has an overdraft this will clearly increase when outgoings in a given period exceed receipts and decrease when receipts exceed outgoings. By making a forecast of these cash flows a businessman can estimate the maximum facility that he is likely to require.

For an existing business the projection may be based on the actual cash flow for the previous year but in the case of a new project the forecast will have to be based on logic, research and experience.

Although the cash flow forecast is in theory a vitally significant document, it contains so many variables that it is difficult to gauge its accuracy. For this reason it has taken the clearing banks many years to accept it as a useful tool. Also for this reason there will always be two sorts of cash flow projection: the one that the businessman prepares for his own use and the one that he prepares for his bank.

A businessman may falsify the projection in such a way as to overestimate his borrowing requirement, either in order to skim off the surplus funds for himself or for another project, or to make it appear that he is contributing more to the project than is actually the case. Or he might underestimate, either to come down to a financial limit imposed by his bank in the hope that he can struggle along somehow, or to come down to a financial limit imposed by his bank in the hope that once they are hooked they will have no choice but to put up further funds as needed in order to protect their original investment.

In Part III of this chapter we met Mr X. Mr X needs to renew his overdraft facility and, working from the previous year's profit and loss account, has made a budget forecast for his own use and a second more optimistic forecast to present to his bank (see Table F).

He now needs to make a cash flow forecast for the year ahead and, working from what he believes to be the accurate budget projection, produces Table G.

1. Opening balance. It is January and Mr X is already £10,000 overdrawn at the bank. So that is the opening balance for the first month of the projection. The opening balance for each succeeding month is carried forward from the closing balance for each month previous.

2. Purchases. Mr X considers that during the course of the year he will actually pay out £30,000 for materials, the monthly figure increasing towards the end of the year when the company is busiest.

3. Wages. In his budget Mr X forecast wages of £35,000 and again the monthly payment will increase as the year goes on and business increases.

4. Overheads are fairly steady but jump every quarter when rent and rates are due.

5. Interest is debited twice yearly.

7. Receipts will be fairly high in January and February as payments are received for goods sold the previous Christmas. After that Mr X knows that receipts will tail away until business improves again the following autumn. Total receipts for the year are expected to be £103,000 on turnover of £110,000, the rest of the money being received in January and February of the following year. Receipts for goods delivered at the end of the previous year will not counterbalance as turnover that year was only £100,000.

8. Net cash flow. By deducting forecast monthly outgoings from forecast monthly receipts Mr X is able to estimate the net amount that will flow into or out of the company's coffers each month.

72

Table G

Cash Flow Forecast based on Budget Projection (Table F, column 2) showing a Maximum Facility Requirement of £27,250 with a Negative Cash Flow for the Year

£000s	Jan	Feb	Mar	Apr	May	June	July	Aug	Sept	Oct	Nov	Dec
1. Opening Balance (OD)*	10	9	8.5	11.5	17	18.5	22.25	27.25	26	22.75	19.5	12.75
2. Purchases	2	2	2	2	2	2	3	3	3	3	3	3
3. Wages	2	2	2.5	2.5	3	3	3	3	3	3.5	3.5	4
4. Overheads	4	2.5	2.5	4	2.5	2.5	4	2.75	2.75	4.25	2.75	2.75
5. Interest						1.25						1.75
6. Total outgoings	8	6.5	7	8.5	7.5	8.75	10	8.75	8.75	10.75	9.25	11.5
7. Receipts	9	7	4	3	6	5	5	10	12	14	16	12
8. Net cash flow	+1	+0.5	-3	-5.5	-1.5	-3.75	-5	+1.25	+3.25	+3.25	+6.75	+0.5
9. Closing balance (OD)*	9	8.5	11.5	17	18.5	22.25	27.25	26	22.75	19.5	12.75	12.25

* overdrawn

73

9. Closing balance is the overdraft figure at the end of the month.

Note: A cash flow forecast may be produced in which opening and closing balances are omitted; the forecast will then simply show the net flow of cash into or out of the business in each period.

From the cash flow forecast Mr X can see that he has two problems. The first is that he needs an overdraft facility of £27,250 (July/August) while his bank manager has already intimated that the maximum that will be allowed is £25,000. By taking longer to settle bills and delaying his production push Mr X believes he can get down to that figure. The second problem is that over the year as a whole the cash flow is negative (the overdraft is £10,000 at the start of the year and £12,250 at the end). The bank will want to see an overall positive flow so that they may be reassured that the company will eventually have the capability to repay the loan entirely. Again, by delaying settling accounts Mr X believes he can meet that requirement. He amends his own cash flow forecast accordingly and then prepares a second for the bank based on his 'manipulated' budget (Table F, column 3), which will meet the bank's criteria.

Mr X presents the cash flow projection in Table H to his bank. The manager notes that the company can operate within a facility of £25,000. He also sees that over the course of the year the company reduces the hard core overdraft from £10,000 to nearly £5,000. Mr X gets his facility.

V THE TECHNIQUES OF FINANCIAL CONTROL

Were you surprised to discover, when your accountant examined your books last, that you had made a loss? Then you are a fool – not because you made a loss, but because you did not know you were making a loss.

That annual profit and loss account is a document produced solely for the benefit of others. If you are losing money now, this month, you need to know by next month at the latest. If the first you know of it is from an accountant a year from now then it is probable that your next instruction to him will be to appoint him liquidator.

To control your business you must produce management

Table H

Cash Flow Forecast based on Manipulated Budget (Table F, column 3) showing a Maximum Facility Requirement of £25,000 with a Positive Cash Flow for the Year

£000s	Jan	Feb	Mar	Apr	May	June	July	Aug	Sept	Oct	Nov	Dec
1. Opening Balance (OD)*	10	9	8.5	11.5	17	18	21.25	25	23.75	18.75	14	6.75
2. Purchases	2	2	2	2	2	2	2	3	3	3	4	3
3. Wages	2	2	2.5	2.5	2.5	2.5	2.75	3	3.25	4	4	4
4. Overheads	4	2.5	2.5	4	2.5	2.5	4	2.75	2.75	4.25	2.75	2.75
5. Interest						1.25						1.75
6. Total outgoings	8	6.5	7	8.5	7	8.25	8.75	8.75	9	11.25	10.75	11.5
7. Receipts	9	7	4	3	6	5	5	10	14	16	18	13
8. Net cash flow	+1	+0.5	-3	-5.5	-1	-3.25	-3.75	+1.25	+5	+4.75	+7.25	+1.5
9. Closing balance (OD)*	9	8.5	11.5	17	18	21.25	25	23.75	18.75	14	6.75	5.25

* overdrawn

75

accounts monthly so that you can take prompt action to correct any problems that they reveal. And you must have at least the capability to extract the necessary information for yourself so that from time to time you can check figures presented to you. Otherwise you will be totally reliant on employees for vital management information. That is a position the smaller businessman cannot allow himself to be in. You will be cheated and never know it.

Management Accounts

THE INFORMATION YOU NEED

Every month you will need to extract orders placed with suppliers; orders placed by customers; goods received; invoices received; other overheads incurred; invoices sent out; total of debtors; total of creditors; bank position; stock figures, either from control sheets or by physical count; payments out; receipts; and production figures.

Micro-computers are now within the reach of many small businesses. They can be programmed not only to print statements, payrolls etc., but also to produce vital management information virtually instantaneously.

SALES PROSPECTS

A simple comparison between orders placed for the month this year with the corresponding period in the previous year will reveal the trend. You should also endeavour to discover whether the market as a whole is expanding or declining and whether your share of that market is increasing or falling.

Action

Possession of figures does not in itself make a business successful. You must consider how increased sales will affect production and finance and plan accordingly. You must consider why sales are falling, what can be done to reverse the trend and what the business can do meanwhile to defend itself.

STOCK CONTROL

You must have a system that will enable you to see the movement of goods into and out of stock, that will give a stock total

for each item and a total value for all stock. In some businesses
this will be easy to achieve; in others, particularly the larger
manufacturing companies, it will be a complex task. But it
must be done. Not only are the figures vital for the monthly assessment of profitability, but they are essential in themselves so
that the efficiency of stock control can be assessed. It is no good
having a year's stock of one of your products and only a week's
supply of another. Equally, you cannot wait to re-order a component until an employee reports that you are out of stock of it.
You must fix a minimum stock quantity at which you will re-
order.

Stock records must be backed up by physical counts at least
twice a year.

CASH FLOW

You will need to compare cash flow with projections previously
made for the period (see Table J) and you will need to revise
projections for the future.

In month 1 actual payments out exceed the forecast while receipts are below forecast. In month 2 the trend continues and

Table J

£000s	Month 1	Month 2	Month 3
Cash Flow Forecast			
Opening balance (OD)*	10	11	10
Payments out	6	7	9
Receipts	5	8	10
Cash flow	-1	+1	+1
Closing balance (OD)*	11	10	9
Actual Cash Flow			
Opening balance (OD)*	10	13	15
Payments out	7	8	5
Receipts	4	6	9
Cash flow	-3	-2	+4
Closing balance (OD)*	13	15	11

* overdrawn

the company is overdrawn at the bank £5,000 more than antici-
pated.

Action
You hold up payments to suppliers and take a strong line with
debtors. The cash flow improves in month 3. You now have to
examine the fundamental cause of cash flow deterioration and
make a revised projection. In making it you will be able to take
into account orders placed with suppliers and by customers for
future delivery, while totals for debtors and creditors will give
an accurate picture of pressures on short-term liquidity.

Failure to meet the forecast might be caused by a decline in
sales, or perhaps you are losing money?

PROFITABILITY
You must compare monthly totals with the budget forecast for
the year:

Table K

£000s	Budget for the year	Month 1	Month 2	Month 3
Sales	100	5	7	9
Purchases	30	4	3	3
Wages	30	2	3	3
Telephone	1	—	—	0.4
Postage	1	0.1	0.1	0.1
etc . . .				

Comparison with the previous year to establish a pattern will
make the monthly figures more meaningful. You now have only
to insert opening and closing stock figures to produce a full
profit and loss account.

As an alternative you may occasionally find it helpful to approach profits by inserting the latest figures into the old balance
sheet.

Table L compares (in a simplified form) figures from a
company's last balance sheet with the latest figures. On the
capital employment side, total net assets are down from
£70,000 to £63,000 and if there have been no other changes on
the capital employed side, the only explanation is that a loss of
£7,000 has been made since the balance sheet date.

Table L

£000s	Balance sheet	Latest figures
Fixed assets	50	48
Debtors	30	25
Stock	40	35
	70	60
Creditors	20	20
Bank overdraft	30	25
	50	45
Net current assets	20	15
Total net assets	70	63
Capital employed		
Shares capital	25	25
Reserves	35	35
Profit	10	?

Action

The Table K approach will reveal the cause of a fall in profits, whether due to a rise in overheads, in which case it will show which particular overheads are to blame, or to a fall in gross margin. If the latter, you will have to consider increasing prices, cutting raw material costs, and how to improve productivity.

But do not assume that identification of the cause of failure will always enable you to reverse the trend; your product may no longer be viable.

The Evaluation of Capital Expenditure

There is controversy amongst businessmen over the analysis of capital projects. On the one hand are those who advocate scientific analysis based on discounted cash flow projections. On the other are the businessmen who argue that accurate prediction of profits five or ten years ahead is impossible and that precise analysis of such projections is therefore pointless.

In fact all methods of evaluation (and the smaller businessman will be using one of them whether he is aware of what it is called or not) are based on very simple concepts.

Pay-back

A machine is worn out. If the businessman wishes to continue in business he must either replace it or employ two additional staff.

Cost of machine	£30,000
Saving in wages	£6,000 per annum
Pay-back period	5 years
Life of machine	10 years

The businessman gets his money back in five years and then enjoys a further five years with a cost saving totalling £30,000.

Return on capital
Average capital employed on a three-year project is £10,000. Profits are £1,000 in the first year, £2,000 in the second and £3,000 in the third.

Average capital	£10,000
Total profit	£6,000
Average annual profit	£2,000
Rate of return	20%

Discounted cash flow
This is the technique that has aroused controversy.

A businessman has two machines to consider, both costing £5,000, having a life of ten years and producing total profits in that period of £10,000. Profits from the first machine run at £2,000 per annum during the first three years, £1,000 per annum for the next two and £400 per annum thereafter. Profits from the second machine run at £1,000 per annum.

Which proposition is best?

Congratulations; you have just used the principle of discounted cash flow to decide that the first machine is best. It gives the same total profit as the second machine, the same average annual profit, but it gives it quicker.

Obvious? Certainly. Controversial? Not at all.

But there is just a little more to it. The basis of discounted cash flow is that because money has a time value (£100 today could be invested to become £110 next year), then the future financial return on an investment must be discounted back to

80

Table M

First Machine

Year	Net cash flow	Discounting factor	Present Value
1	£ 2,000	0.909091	£1,818
2	2,000	0.826446	1,652
3	2,000	0.751315	1,502
4	1,000	0.683013	683
5	1,000	0.620921	620
6	400	0.564474	225
7	400	0.513158	205
8	400	0.466507	186
9	400	0.424098	169
10	400	0.385543	154
	£10,000		£7,214

Second Machine

Year	Net cash flow	Discounting factor	Present Value
1	£ 1,000	0.909091	£ 909
2	1,000	0.826446	826
3	1,000	0.751315	751
4	1,000	0.683013	683
5	1,000	0.620921	620
6	1,000	0.564474	564
7	1,000	0.513158	513
8	1,000	0.466507	466
9	1,000	0.424098	424
10	1,000	0.385543	385
	£10,000		£6,141

the time the investment was made. The economists set it out as above.

The first machine is clearly the better proposition because when profits are discounted back they exceed those produced by the second machine by over £1,000.

The *discounting factor* in Table M is based on a rate of 10 per cent. The businessman considers that if he has £909.09 today he can invest it to produce £1,000 in a year's time. Compound interest is involved in the calculation of the discounting factor for each year after the first; the businessman would be well advised to buy a set of tables.

Each businessman will have to make his own decision on the rate at which he will discount back. If he is borrowing he can discount back on the basis of the rate of interest he is paying.

EXAMPLE: A businessman borrows on overdraft at 10 per cent. He calculates that at the end of one year he will receive a profit of £600, which he has to discount back. He knows that for every £100 borrowed the bank will want £110 in one year, therefore he must discount back at 100 divided by 110, a factor of 0.909091. At 15 per cent he would discount back at 100 divided by 115, a factor of 0.869565.

USEFUL BOOKS

Hall, A. G., *An Introduction to Modern Book-Keeping* (Heinemann, 1974)
Lee, G. A., *Modern Financial Accounting* (Nelson, 1973)
Rundle, Cyril, *Accountancy for Everyone* (David & Charles, 1977)
Wood, Frank, *Business Accounting* (Longman, 1972)

4

TAKEOVERS

In which we consider buying and selling businesses.

A takeover may have any or all of the following aims:

1. Entry into a new area of business without the problems of beginning from scratch.

2. The rationalisation of two or more similar or complementary businesses, for example where two factories making similar products are combined (horizontal integration) or where a manufacturing company takes over a retail outlet (vertical integration).

3. The gaining of a larger market share. Once a company holds a significant share of a market it can begin to influence taste, fashion and prices.

4. The acquisition of assets at below their true value.

5. The creation of a conglomerate whose worth exceeds the sum of its parts. A common device is to reverse a number of private companies into a public company shell, the public company status conferring a vastly increased value on them.

However, takeovers often have disastrous results:

1. The merging of two successful companies into one inefficient loss-maker.

2. Loss to the shareholders of the target company.

3. Loss to the shareholders of the purchasing company or to individuals making a purchase.

The businessman has to face the evidence of analysts in the public company field that the majority of mergers, while benefiting individuals, have been damaging to the companies concerned. There are also casualties at the bottom of the ladder.

EXAMPLE: Mr H—— was a unit trust salesman and before that a bank manager. He and his wife decided to buy a village store. The figures provided by the vendor were impressive, the H——s paid £6,000 for the lease, bought the stock and moved in.

Turnover was far below expectations and they were advised that they had a case for misrepresentation. But it was seven years before the courts awarded them £15,000; the vendor's assets realised only £5,300.

The truth is that takeover is a much abused and indeed misunderstood weapon; like any tool it has to be used correctly. In the case of Mr H—— his own words underline his mistake: 'It only took a day to realise I had been caught.' That was a day he should have taken before he signed the contract, not after.

Finding a Buyer/Seller

An active seller will advertise – the *Financial Times* is good for all categories, the *Daily Telegraph* for hotels, restaurants etc; reply to advertisements placed by those wishing to buy; approach companies that might be assumed to be interested; and instruct brokers.

An active buyer may advertise; contact companies in the field in which he is interested; and contact brokers.

Mechanics of Takeover   *problems 44–52*

PURCHASE BY SHARES

The purchase of a company by shares has the following advantages:

1. The acquisition of an existing track record and established creditworthiness.

2. Continuity.

3. Lower initial outlay.

EXAMPLE: A company's assets are factory £50,000, stock £30,000, debtors £15,000. Liabilities are bank overdraft £22,000, mortgage £20,000, creditors £20,000. Total assets of £95,000 are therefore balanced by liabilities of £62,000, so that the price paid for shares will reflect a net asset value of £33,000. But to purchase the factory and the stock on their own would involve an outlay of £80,000.

The disadvantages are as follows:

1. The purchaser may be obliged to pay for assets that he does not require.

2. The company may have undisclosed liabilities and contingent liabilities.

3. As a result of item 2 above a detailed contract with warranties will be required and this will involve considerable expense.

4. There may be financing and legal difficulties revolving around Section 54 of the Companies Act 1948 (see below).

The law

As regards private companies the law on takeover by share transfer is simple, but the implications are great – see items 2 and 3 above. It is essential that the basically simple transfer of shares is accompanied by a contract stating the conditions under which the purchase is made and containing warranties by the vendors. The purchaser should be alive to the possibility of retaining part of the purchase price against any breach (the seller should resist).

The most significant rule of law is contained in Section 54 of the Companies Act 1948, which makes it illegal for a limited company to deal in its own shares, to give or loan money to enable its shares to be purchased or to give a guarantee or mortgage to enable money to be borrowed for the purchase of its shares.

The criminal penalties for infringement are small and doubtless there are many more breaches of Section 54 than prosecutions. As regards civil penalties, any shareholders or creditors of the company who suffer loss as a result of breach of Section 54 may sue for damages.

PURCHASE BY ASSETS

Purchase of assets is the only way of acquiring unincorporated businesses and companies may also be purchased in this way.

It has the following advantages:

1. It is easier for the purchaser to select what assets will and will not be included.

2. The purchaser will not be liable for the debts of the seller.

3. The contract for the purchase will be simpler and therefore less costly.

4. Section 54 of the Companies Act 1948 is avoided, making financing easier.

5. The profits of asset stripping accrue directly to the purchaser and do not remain within a company taken over.

The disadvantages are as follows:

1. No track record is acquired – no accounts, balance sheets, established creditworthiness etc.

2. Loss of continuity.

3. There being no counterbalancing liabilities, the initial outlay for assets only will be high.

TAX NOTES
Sale by shares
Where sale is by shares, a vendor will be liable for capital gains tax, but there may be relief if he is over sixty.

If vendors accept public company shares (or private company shares – but this would not generally be a good idea) in exchange for their own, the tax will be postponed under roll-over provisions until those shares are sold. The tax may be avoided altogether where the vendor of the original shares holds the exchange shares until death. It may be viable to borrow against them, to avoid having to sell them.

Sale by assets
If the vendor has only a small part of the total purchase price attributed to stock he may be able to reduce his profit and therefore his tax liability for the period preceding the sale. The effect on the purchaser will be to make his first-year results look good. However, the purchaser may seek to have a large part of the purchase price attributed to stock in order to reduce his own first-year profit and liability for tax.

On plant, a high figure will allow the purchaser to claim good capital allowances but may cause the vendor to lose some of his.

If a vendor of assets as opposed to shares takes shares in exchange, then the roll-over provisions will apply as above.

Valuing a Business

Mr G—— had built up his import/export business from nothing in 1950 to a turnover of £250,000 by 1975. His judgement was good; he knew how to pick a winner. In 1976 he asked his bank for finance to launch a new product, but it flopped.

G—— felt sure that he could recover if only he could conceal the truth from his bank for long enough. The first giveaway would be his turnover figures for 1976. At first he fobbed off the bank with his own 'estimates', but when his overdraft refused to come down they insisted on prompt audited accounts. G—— began invoicing 1977 deliveries as if they had been despatched the previous year and made appropriate additions to the books.

That took care of turnover which now looked healthy.

But still something more was needed to help profits. G——— applied the same procedure to his creditors, but in reverse. He removed all record of certain debts that were outstanding at the end of 1976, selecting only those creditors who would be unknown to his accountant – the accountant would not know of their existence, let alone cross-check them when he made his audit.

The auditor produced accounts showing a healthy profit and the bank was temporarily appeased. But G——— had only transferred his problems from 1976 to 1977. What next?

He decided to sell out.

From a company file at Companies House, London or Cardiff, a businessman may obtain information about profitability; net asset value; whether or not premises are freehold; charges on the company's assets; and shareholders and directors.

Once negotiations have been opened, an intending purchaser will require profit and loss accounts and balance sheets for three to five years; access to the books; costings; customer lists; product samples; stock valuation; valuation of fixed asscts; market survey; assessment of the stability of supply of raw materials; and details of employees.

A certain amount of information can be obtained without disruption and in secrecy, but a point will inevitably be reached when the seller will begin to worry, firstly that he is giving away confidential data that might enable the intending purchaser to set up in competition, and secondly that the negotiations will become known and have a detrimental effect on relations with staff, customers and suppliers. For his part the intending purchaser must allow for genuine reluctance on these grounds on the part of the seller, but he must also take heed of the fact that such reluctance may simply be a shield behind which to hide disagreeable facts. Inevitably a point will be reached where the purchaser threatens, 'Either you provide me with the information I need or the deal is off.'

One way of reducing friction is to agree not a price but a formula for agreeing a price. The parties may then sign a contract embodying this formula and the actual purchase price may then be calculated on the day of takeover, although this will not, of course, obviate the need for confidential pre-contract information altogether.

EXAMPLE: When P—— made a bid for N—— L—— Ltd it was agreed that trading stocks would be valued at list selling price less 40 per cent, that slow-moving or redundant stocks would be valued at list selling price less 65 per cent and that part of the purchase price would be set aside for payment to the seller or repayment to the purchaser in accordance with turnover in the year following takeover.

A business has no definitive value. At best there is a rule of thumb against which buyer and seller can measure how well or how badly they have done.

The general rules for a buyer are simple:

1. Never take the audited profit and loss accounts and balance sheets at face value (see Chapter Three, and remember Mr G—— above).

2. Never assess the price of a private company in accordance with the criteria for a public company. It is the fact that there is a market in public company shares but not in private company shares that causes the difference, and it is by taking advantage of this that the wheeling-dealing businessman makes instant profits by reversing private companies into public companies.

3. Never value goodwill in accordance with some fixed formula such as 'three years' profits'. The price for goodwill has to do with the difference between the profits the company makes and the profits the businessman would make if he invested his money elsewhere.

EXAMPLE: A retail shop has net assets of £40,000 and profits of £10,000 per annum. The accountant for the shareholders claims a price of £40,000 plus three years' profits (£30,000) making a total of £70,000. It might be inferred from that formula that the £40,000 for net assets entitles the purchaser to no profit and that only the extra £30,000 obtains profits – which is absurd. The purchaser calculates that if he invests £40,000 into opening a brand-new shop he can expect first-year profits of £6,000, which means that the accountant has just asked him to pay £30,000 for an additional £4,000 profit.

4. Never pay twice for goodwill.

EXAMPLES:

(a) H—— bought a shop, paying £6,000 for the lease (which had four years to run before review at about £2,000 below the market rent) and £6,000 for the £2,000 a year profit. He overlooked the fact that the £2,000 a year profit and the £2,000 a year saving in rent were one and the same thing.

(b) P—— bought a manufacturing company that had its own freehold premises valued at £75,000 by the directors. P—— thought he was being rather clever because he knew the factory was worth at least £90,000. Profits were running at £13,000 per annum and on the basis of that P—— paid £30,000 for goodwill. But in fact the company's profit was entirely dependent upon the fact that it occupied its own premises for which it allowed no rent and on which there was no mortgage. The trading profit of the company was only £4,000.

5. Never value on the basis of the future profits that *you* will generate.

6. Never confuse executive directors' emoluments or working proprietors' income with profits. Profits are what is left after the directors/proprietors have been satisfied. You do not have to buy an income for yourself, which is what you will be doing if you ignore this. You can earn a living without investing a penny, and it is called working for someone else. If a business has no profit after allowing an income for the businessman, then it has no profit.

7. Always ensure that you get a good return on capital invested (see Chapter Three). There is no point in paying £10,000 for a machine, albeit it cost £20,000 new the year before, if it can only earn you £5 a week.

8. Always take a pessimistic view. Be like a banker. In fact you can do no better than to take the accounts to a bank and ask for a loan on the strength of them, whether you really want it or not. If you want to hear a ruthless valuation, you'll hear it from the bank.

PROBLEMS AND SOLUTIONS

44. I have been given the audited accounts for the past year for a company I wish to take over. Can I rely upon them?
No. Furthermore, the accounts for only one year are insufficient (see Chapter Three).

45. I am having difficulty getting finance for a takeover.
There is no special source of finance for takeovers. For general sources see Chapter Two.

Have you considered that your difficulty may arise because you are paying too much? If the problem derives from the fact that you are buying shares and risk infringing Section 54, then consider buying assets only. It is often necessary to strip out assets and if you can see a profitable way of doing this you may be able to convert part of your financing requirement into a bridging loan, which should be relatively easy to arrange. But remember that if a limited company is involved the proceeds of stripping must remain inside the company; they help finance the running of the company but not its purchase. Try also getting the vendors to accept payments spread over several years.

46. I have been offered a substantial sum for my business but the payment is to be spread over five years. I do not need all the money at once so would this be a good idea?
No. Quite apart from the security aspect it is all too easy for a purchaser to find grounds why payment should be either stopped or reduced. To enforce your rights may take years, if not prove impossible. Also, it may be inferred that the purchasers are short of cash and intend to pay you out of profits, which is both illegal and, from your point of view, risky. What happens if profits fall? Only accept as a last resort, and if you do so ensure that you have ample security and that the purchasers can have no grounds for withholding later payments. Also, consider that you will want much more spread over five years than you would accept in cash today (see 'Discounted cash flow', pp. 80–2).

47. I have taken over a business, paying half the agreed price at the outset with the balance payable at the end of the first year. I have not been doing the amount of business I was led to expect and feel justified in keeping part of the money back. Can I do this?
You start from a position of strength because you already have the money, which is one of the remedies for misrepresentation. The other is rescission – that is, both parties are restored to their positions prior to the takeover (see Chapter Five on contract).

48. How can I protect myself in making an offer for a business against misrepresentation by the vendors?
The law does provide remedies (see above and Chapter Five), and to facilitate their use you should ensure that all relevant representations are made by the vendors in writing and make it

clear that your offer is influenced by them. However, as it is always best to ensure that you are not defrauded rather than look to see what you can do about it after the event, you should investigate all claims until you are satisfied. Withhold part of the purchase price against loss through misrepresentation.

49. I have agreed a price for a company based upon a profit and loss account and balance sheet drawn up about three months ago. How can I ensure that the directors do not remove assets – for example by selling them off for cash – prior to the takeover date next month?
Never agree a price on the basis of figures that are even three months out of date, nor where they have been prepared by anyone other than yourself or your advisers. Net asset value must be determined on the day of purchase; all you can do now is agree a formula for valuation.

50. How can I ensure that the vendors of a business which I am buying do not set up in competition with me?
Make their undertaking not to do so a condition of your agreement to purchase, by inserting a restraint clause. But note that restraints are void unless it can be shown that they are reasonable in the circumstances (see Chapter Five).

51. I held half the shares in a private company but recently acquired the remainder from my co-director who decided to retire. The auditors say I have contravened Section 54 of the Companies Act 1948 because I made myself a loan from the company in order to pay for the shares. But I cannot see that it matters as I am now the only significant shareholder.
This section of the Companies Act protects creditors as well as shareholders from the diminution of the company's worth by its buying or loaning money for the purchase of its own shares. The criminal penalty is small but creditors who lose money as a result of the infringement may sue. Doubtless the auditors will be prepared for you to restore the position by repaying the money or, possibly, if the sum involved is not too large, you may put it down as salary.

52. If I buy the assets of a limited company what happens about the name?

91

The company whose assets you are buying can apply for a new name. You may then either register the old name as the property of your company or change the name of your company to the name you intend acquiring.

USEFUL BOOKS AND ADDRESSES

Davis, William, *Merger Mania* (Constable, 1970)
McKnight, Gerald, *The Fortune Makers* (Michael Joseph, 1972)

To research companies: Companies House, Crown Way, Maindy, Cardiff CF4 3QZ; or Companies House, 55 City Road, London EC1Y 1BB

5

DISPUTES OVER CONTRACTS AND THE SALE OF GOODS

In which we consider who may enforce a contract; disputes over terms; what makes an apparent contract void, an actual contract voidable or unenforceable; how a contract is frustrated; how an innocent party may be discharged by time; and remedies.

Who May Enforce a Contract? *problem 53*

Only those party to a contract may enforce it.

EXAMPLE: *Dunlop Pneumatic Tyre Co Ltd* v. *Selfridge & Co Ltd* (1915). Selfridge & Co bought tyres from a wholesaler undertaking not to resell them at below the manufacturer's list price. Dunlop, the manufacturers, sued Selfridge for breach when the list price was ignored. The action failed because, although Dunlop had contracted with the wholesaler, they were not party to the contract between the wholesaler and Selfridge.

Another way of expressing this doctrine of privity is that a person seeking to enforce a contract must have provided consideration and must not be merely a beneficiary (see 'No consideration', pp. 97–8). The exceptions are as follows:

1. A principal is automatically party to a contract made on his behalf by an agent (see 'Commission agents', pp. 131–3).

2. Certain existing covenants will remain enforceable by the new owner when land is sold or by a new tenant when a lease is assigned.

3. A third party may sue under an insurance policy from which he stands to benefit – for example, a person who is injured in a motor accident.

4. A third party may be able to sue over a cheque or a bill of exchange.

Disputes over the Terms of a Contract

A contract is a legally binding agreement between two or more persons and except in certain circumstances (see pp. 103–4) is no less a contract because it is oral rather than in writing.

EXPRESS TERMS
Express terms are those incorporated into a contract.

IMPLIED TERMS
In certain circumstances terms that are not incorporated into a contract may be implied.

Custom
Provided they are not contrary to express terms, the customs of the particular trade concerned may be implied into a contract.
  EXAMPLE: *Smith* v. *Wilson* (1832). It was held that the words 'one thousand rabbits' in a contract actually meant 1,200 rabbits under local custom.

Efficacy
The court will imply terms to give efficacy to a contract.
  EXAMPLE: *The Moorcock* (1889). It was held that where there was a contract for a vessel called the *Moorcock* to unload at a jetty, there was an implied term that it would be safe to berth there.

Sale of goods
The following terms are implied under the Sale of Goods Act 1893 as amended by the Supply of Goods (Implied Terms) Act 1973:
  1. The vendor has the right to sell the goods. Full disclosure must be made of any charges on the goods.
  2. The goods will correspond to their description, if sold by description, even if a sample is also produced or the buyer makes his own selection.
  3. The goods will correspond to the sample, if sold by sample, and a defect in the sample which is not apparent upon a reasonable examination does not remove liability from the vendor for that defect in the bulk.
  4. The goods will be of merchantable quality, if purchased from a dealer, except where defects have been pointed out or the goods were examined by the purchaser to whom the defects should have been obvious.

5. The goods will be fit for the purpose intended, if purchased from a dealer, provided either that the purpose is obvious from the goods or that the purpose was made known to the dealer.

Exemption clauses

In consumer sales, liability under implied terms may not be excluded even by express agreement. In non-consumer sales the seller must always have the right to sell but other implied terms may be avoided by agreement and provided that it is fair and reasonable that the seller should avoid liability under them. A consumer sale is one in which, in the course of business, the seller sells goods of a type ordinarily bought for private use to a purchaser who does not buy, or hold himself out as buying, in the course of business.

UNFAIR TERMS

The Unfair Contract Terms Act 1977 limited 'the extent to which . . . civil liability for breach of contract, or for negligence or other breach of duty, can be avoided by means of contract terms and otherwise'.

The Act came into force on 1 February 1978 and generally makes invalid any terms in a contract which unreasonably restrict liability for negligence for loss or damage; restrict liability for negligence for death or injury; or restrict liability for misrepresentation or remove the remedy for misrepresentation. (The Act must be read in conjunction with the Misrepresentation Act 1967.)

TRADE DESCRIPTIONS ACT 1968

The Act makes it a criminal offence in the course of business to apply false trade descriptions to goods or to supply or offer to supply goods falsely described.

The Criminal Justice Act 1972 allows the court to make compensation orders to the victims of a false trade description.

The accused has a valid defence if he can prove that the false trade description was a mistake or beyond his control or due to incorrect information given to him, provided that he also proves that he was not negligent.

PAROL

While there is a presumption in favour of written contracts being comprehensive, evidence of additional oral terms to a contract will be admitted by the court in certain circumstances.

EXAMPLES:

Pym v. *Campbell* (1856). It was held that a partnership agreement would not come into effect until an invention had been patented, this being an oral condition precedent.

Quickmaid Rental Services v. *Reece* (1970). It was held that an agreement to hire a vending machine was voidable upon another machine being installed in the same road, an oral assurance having been given by the salesman that this would not be permitted. The oral assurance was considered to have formed part of the contract.

Is the Contract Void?

An apparent contract is void – that is, no contract in fact exists – if it lacks some essential that would make it a contract in the eyes of the law; infringes the law; involves certain types of mistake; is made by a company acting *ultra vires*; or, being of a particular type, is made with a minor.

NO OFFER AND ACCEPTANCE   *problem 54*

A contract is void unless an offer has been made and accepted.

An offer has the following features:

1. It is a statement by one party that he is willing to be bound to certain terms.

2. The display of goods in a shop or in an advertisement is not an offer but an invitation to treat.

HOWEVER: *Carlill* v. *Carbolic Smoke Ball Co* (1892). It was held that an offer in an advertisement by the Carbolic Smoke Ball Co to pay £100 to anyone who used the ball and then caught influenza was binding because in this case the offer contained a statement making it clear that the defendants were willing to be bound.

3. An offer may be revoked at any time prior to acceptance (but see *Byrne* v. *Van Tienhoven* below) provided that there was no promise to keep the offer open for a specified time either under seal or by the acceptance of consideration by the offeree.

4. An offer lapses when it is either rejected or not accepted within the specified time or within a reasonable time.

Acceptance has the following features:

1. It occurs when the party to whom the offer was made agrees to its terms precisely.

2. A qualified acceptance is in fact a counter-offer causing the original offer to lapse.

3. Except where goods are requested on approval, silence cannot constitute acceptance.

EXAMPLE: *Felthouse* v. *Bindley* (1862). Felthouse wrote to his nephew: 'If I hear no more about him, I consider the horse is mine at £30 15s.' Although his nephew did not reply, it was held that his silence was not acceptance.

4. Under the Unsolicited Goods and Services Act 1971 it is a criminal offence to demand payment for unsolicited goods that have not been accepted. Silence on the part of the recipient does not constitute acceptance (see item 3 above). The recipient of unsolicited goods may take the goods as a gift after six months if the sender does not repossess them; take the goods as a gift if the sender does not repossess them after having been given thirty days' written notice of the recipient's intention; or contract to purchase the goods.

The case of Byrne v. Van Tienhoven (1880)
On 1 October Van Tienhoven in Cardiff posted an offer to Byrne in New York. He then changed his mind and on 8 October posted a letter of revocation. On 11 October Byrne received the letter of offer and telegraphed acceptance; he did not receive the letter of revocation until the 20th. It was held that the contract was valid from the 11th.

Neither an offer nor a revocation of offer by post can be valid until received, although a contract is made at the moment acceptance is posted.

NO INTENTION TO CREATE LEGAL RELATIONS
A contract is void unless the parties intend to create legal relations. In commercial matters there is a presumption of such an intention but in social and domestic matters there is no such presumption.

EXAMPLE: *Appleson* v. *Littlewood* (1939). Appleson claimed £4,335 winnings on a football pool. A clause on the coupon stated that neither the sending nor the acceptance of the coupon would give rise to a legal relationship. It was held that the plaintiff could take no action.

NO CONSIDERATION   *problem 55*
With the exception of contracts under seal a contract is void

unless both parties give, or promise to give, consideration.

Consideration has been defined (*Currie* v. *Misa*, 1875) as 'some right, interest, profit or benefit accruing to the one party, or . . . some forbearance, detriment, loss or responsibility given, suffered or undertaken by the other'. (In the case of a guarantee the consideration by the creditor is generally the granting of a loan to the debtor.) For example, where A pays £100 and B supplies goods, both sides have given consideration.

EXAMPLE: *Carlill* v. *Carbolic Smoke Ball Co* (1893). In this case, already described above, the defendants claimed that Mrs Carlill had given no consideration for their promise to pay £100. It was held that the inconvenience of using the smoke ball constituted consideration.

Consideration has the following features:

1. It must be real but it need not be adequate.

EXAMPLES:

(a) W—— agreed to sell a painting for £100, not realising that it was worth over £1,000. The contract was valid.

(b) G—— ordered £5,000 of materials from B—— Ltd. Terms were settlement twenty-eight days. After three months G—— offered £4,000 in full settlement, saying that he was in financial difficulty. B—— Ltd accepted, but a year later successfully sued for the balance. G—— had given no consideration for their agreement to accept less than they were already entitled to.

2. Consideration must not be 'past'.

EXAMPLE: Four factories on a small estate had frontages on to the same service road. Three decided to have the road resurfaced but the fourth refused to contribute. Once the work was complete the managing director of the fourth factory was again pressed to pay part of the cost and agreed. When he failed to do so he was sued, but successfully defended the case. A promise to pay for something only after it has already been done is not enforceable.

ILLEGALITY

Contracts for illegal purposes are void.

Restraints   *problems 56–9*

A contract in restraint of trade is void unless it can be shown that it is reasonable and that it is not against public interest.

Fitch v. *Dewes* (1921). In order to make a test case a solicitor's managing clerk deliberately broke a restraint clause in his contract of employment by practising within seven miles of Tamworth after leaving the solicitor's employment. The restraint was upheld as reasonable and not against public interest.

Provident Clothing & Supply Co Ltd v. *Mason* (1913). A clause in his contract of employment forbade Mason to take a similar job within twenty-five miles of London within three years of leaving the company. Mason took a job with a rival firm immediately upon leaving but an injunction against him was refused on the grounds that the prohibited area was unreasonably large.

MISTAKES   *problems 60–62*

The following mistakes render a contract void:

1. Mistakes as to the nature of the instrument.

EXAMPLE: *Carlisle and Cumberland Banking Co* v. *Bragg* (1911). Bragg was induced to sign a guarantee for a bank overdraft to R——, who told him that it was a contract for insurance. It was held that Bragg was not liable under the guarantee as he was mistaken as to the nature of the document.

BUT: *Saunders* v. *Anglia Building Society* (1971). A woman assigned the lease of her home to her nephew's friend in the belief that it was actually an assignment to her nephew. It was held that the contract was valid because there was no mistake as to the nature of the document.

2. Mistakes as to the identity or existence of the subject-matter.

EXAMPLE: *Raffles* v. *Wichelhaus* (1864). It was held that no contract existed where one party agreed to buy a consignment of cotton aboard a ship called the *Peerless* while the other was referring to another consignment aboard a different vessel also called the *Peerless*.

3. Mutual mistakes going to the root of the contract.

EXAMPLE: *Cooper* v. *Phibbs* (1867). It was held that a lease was void when it was discovered that the lessee was the owner of the property, both parties having believed that it belonged to the lessor.

BUT: *Bell* v. *Lever Bros Ltd* (1932). It was held that an agreement by Lever Bros to pay Bell £30,000 for the cancellation of his service contract was not void when they subsequently discovered that Bell could have been summarily dismissed. Their mistake did not go to the root of the contract as they did obtain cancellation of the service agreement.

4. Mistakes as to the identity of the other party, of which the other party is aware.

EXAMPLE: *Sowler* v. *Potter* (1940). Ann Robinson, having convictions concerning prostitution, applied for and was granted a lease in the name Ann Potter. When the landlord discovered her true identity he obtained a declaration that the lease was void on the grounds of mistaken identity.

BUT: *Lewis* v. *Averay* (1972). A confidence trickster agreed to buy a car from Lewis and then, representing himself as a wealthy and famous actor, offered a cheque, which Lewis accepted. The trickster then sold the car to Averay for cash. When Lewis discovered that the cheque he had been given was worthless, he took action against Averay, the trickster having disappeared. The court held that at the time he sold the car to Averay the trickster was the legal owner of the car. Lewis had agreed to sell to the person physically present and the question of identity was only significant in respect of the decision to accept a cheque. The trickster's contract with Lewis was not void and Averay therefore had a good title. However, it was further held that while the contract was not void it would have been voidable for fraud. It was Lewis's misfortune that he took no steps to avoid the contract prior to Averay making his purchase in good faith. In his summing-up Lord Denning disagreed with the judgement in *Sowler* v. *Potter* above and expressed the opinion that that contract, too, was voidable, not void.

5. Mistakes by one party, of which the other party is aware, as to the terms of the contract.

EXAMPLE: *Webster* v. *Cecil* (1861). Cecil intended to sell a property for £2,250 but mistakenly wrote £1,250 and Webster agreed to buy at that price. Webster was subsequently unable to obtain an order for specific performance because he had been aware of the mistake at the time he agreed to buy.

ULTRA VIRES   *problem 63*

A contract made by a company acting beyond the powers contained in the objects clause of the memorandum (see p. 14) is void, where the other party is aware of the circumstances. But, under the European Communities Act 1972:

1. An *ultra vires* contract cannot be enforced by the company.

2. An *ultra vires* contract can be enforced against the company by the other party acting in good faith.

3. Directors will be liable to their shareholders for losses incurred on *ultra vires* contracts.

MINORS   *problem 64*
Contracts entered into by persons under the age of eighteen are void under the Infants' Relief Act 1874 if they are for the repayment of money or for 'unnecessary' goods or services.

EXAMPLE: *Nash* v. *Inman* (1908). It was held that a tailor could not sue an undergraduate for payment for eleven waistcoats.

Is the Contract Voidable?

A contract is voidable – that is, one party has the option of either affirming or repudiating – where that party lacks contractual capacity; the contract was made as a result of misrepresentation; or there was extreme inequality of bargaining power. A voidable contract is valid unless and until the party entitled to do so treats it as void.

NO CONTRACTUAL CAPACITY
Mental incapacity
Contracts for 'unnecessary' goods or services made by a person who through temporary or permanent mental incapacity was incapable of understanding them are voidable at the option of that person provided the incapacity was apparent to the other party.

Minors
Contracts under which a minor acquires some right of property to which obligations attach – partnership agreement, lease, shares, freehold property – may be repudiated by the minor, but are otherwise binding on both parties.

MISREPRESENTATION   *problem 65*
A contract is voidable at the option of a party who has been influenced by an untrue statement of fact by the other party made outside and prior to the contract and as a result of which he has suffered loss.

EXAMPLE: *Dobell* v. *Stevens* (1825). Dobell purchased the lease of a public house after the defendant had fraudulently

misrepresented the turnover. On discovering the fraud he successfully sued for damages.

Silence will not constitute misrepresentation (*caveat emptor* –
let the buyer beware) unless:

1. It is over a matter on which information has been specifically requested.

2. There has been a change in the position over which a factual statement had previously been made.

3. There is a special relationship between the parties, for
example solicitor/client.

4. The omission of one particular fact gives an untrue picture
of the overall position.

5. The contract is one requiring the 'utmost good faith', for
example insurance contracts, partnership agreements.

EXAMPLE: *With* v. *O'Flanagan* (1936). In January a doctor
stated correctly that his practice was worth £2,000 per annum.
Between January and May, when the contract to sell the practice was signed, it produced only £5 a week. The contract was
set aside on the grounds that the doctor should have reported
the changed circumstances.

INEQUALITY OF BARGAINING POWER   *problem 66*
The case of Lloyds Bank Ltd v Bundy (1975)
Bundy, his son and a company formed by his son all banked at
the same branch of Lloyds. The bank asked Bundy to give a
personal guarantee and a charge over his house as security for
an overdraft to the son's company, which was in financial difficulty. On appeal it was held that the bank had a confidential relationship with Bundy that imposed on them a duty of fiduciary
care. The bank should have told Bundy to seek independent
advice before signing. The personal guarantee and charge were
set aside.

Lord Denning MR opened his remarks with these words:
'Now let me say at once that in the vast majority of cases a customer who signs a bank guarantee or a charge cannot get out of
it.' But he concluded: 'The English law gives relief to one who,
without independent advice, enters into a contract on terms
which are very unfair or transfers property for a consideration
which is grossly inadequate, when his bargaining power is
grievously impaired by reason of his own needs or desires, or by
his own ignorance or infirmity, coupled with undue influences

or pressures brought to bear on him by or for the benefit of the other.'

This is a very significant case, but exactly how far the judgement extends has yet to be tested.

Duress and undue influence

A contract is voidable by the innocent party:

1. Where that party was subject to duress – blackmail, violence etc.

EXAMPLE: *Kaufman* v. *Gerson* (1904). Kaufman threatened Mrs Gerson that he would prosecute her husband unless she herself paid over money that her husband owed him. It was held that Mrs Gerson's agreement could not be enforced, having been obtained under duress.

2. Where that party was subject to undue influence by the other, as in the relationship between parent and child, doctor and patient, solicitor and client, spiritual adviser and follower.

Is the Contract Enforceable?

A contract exists but is not enforceable when it is not in the correct form; because of mutual mistake it does not correctly express the intended terms; or the right of remedy has lapsed by time.

INCORRECT FORM

In certain circumstances a contract is unenforceable unless by deed:

1. In the case of land sales the actual conveyance must be by deed.

2. In the case of the leasing of land the actual lease must be by deed if it is for more than three years.

3. The creation of a legal mortgage must be by deed.

4. A gratuitous promise – that is, one in which one party gives no consideration – will not be enforceable unless by deed.

A contract is unenforceable unless in writing if it is a negotiable instrument; a share transfer; or a contract under the Consumer Credit Act 1974.

An oral contract is unenforceable unless supported by written evidence if it is a guarantee (that is, an agreement to be answerable for the debt, default or miscarriage of another) or for the sale of land – the actual transfer itself must be by deed, of course.

Part performance

In certain disputes where specific performance is sought but where the requirements for written evidence have not been complied with, it may nevertheless be possible to enforce the contract if part performance can be shown.

EXAMPLE: *Rawlinson* v. *Ames* (1925). Mrs Ames orally agreed to take a lease of Mrs Rawlinson's flat, and alterations were made to the flat by Mrs Rawlinson at the request of Mrs Ames. It was held that the alterations constituted an act of part performance and that the oral contract between Mrs Ames and Mrs Rawlinson was enforceable.

MISTAKE IN EXPRESSION

A contract is not enforceable where, owing to a mutual and significant mistake, it does not correctly express the intention of the parties.

LIMITATION ACTS 1939–75

No action may be commenced after six years for 'simple' contracts or after twelve years for contracts under seal, the time to run from the date of the breach or, in the case of fraud, from the date of discovery.

But the right of action may be revived by a written acknowledgement of a debt.

EXAMPLE: *Jones* v. *Bellgrove Properties Ltd* (1949). An action in 1947 for the recovery of money borrowed in 1936–7 was allowed although outside the six-year period because the defendant had acknowledged the debt by making provision for it in balance sheets from 1939 to 1945.

COLLECTIVE BARGAINING AGREEMENT

A collective bargaining agreement is not enforceable unless it is in writing and contains a clause stating that it may be enforced.

Has the Contract Been Frustrated?

Both parties to a contract are discharged from their obligations where certain significant and unforeseen events occur, such as a change in the law making the contract illegal; death or illness, in personal service contracts; or destruction of the basis of the contract.

CHANGE OF LAW
A contract is frustrated if it is legal when made but becomes illegal as a result of a change in the law or in other circumstances.

EXAMPLE: *Zinc Corporation Ltd* v. *Hirsch* (1916). It was held that a ten-year contract to supply zinc to a German business was frustrated by the outbreak of war in 1914, as it would mean supplying an enemy alien.

DEATH OR ILLNESS
A personal service contract is frustrated by death or illness.

EXAMPLE: *Robinson* v. *Davison* (1871). It was held that a contract for Robinson to play at a concert was frustrated by her illness.

DESTRUCTION OF BASIS OF CONTRACT
A contract is frustrated when some unforeseen event occurs to destroy the whole basis of the agreement, provided neither party is responsible.

EXAMPLE: *Howell* v. *Coupland* (1876). It was held that a contract to sell a specific crop of potatoes was frustrated when the crop was destroyed by disease, without any negligence on the part of the grower.

BUT: *Monkland* v. *Jack Barclay Ltd* (1951). It was held that a contract to sell a (non-specific) Bentley Mark VI was not frustrated when the motor dealer was unable to obtain such a car for his customer.

Davis Contractors Ltd v. *Fareham UDC* (1956). It was held that a building contract was not frustrated merely because it had become unprofitable.

Has the Contract Been Performed in Time? *problem 67*
The innocent party to a contract is discharged from his obligations where the other party does not perform his part on the day specified or within the time specified or, there being no time stipulated in the contract, within a reasonable time. But time is not of the essence in contracts for the sale of land unless the

contract expressly provides otherwise, and a date may be waived by the court if it appears that the parties did not intend that the date should be strictly observed.

Disputes over Title to Goods

HAS TITLE TO GOODS PASSED? *problems 68, 69*
The exact moment at which title to goods is transferred under a contract may be of critical importance where, for example, they are damaged or destroyed or the purchaser becomes insolvent.

1. Title to goods passes at such time as the contract states or implies that it will pass. But where no intention is apparent:

2. Title to goods that the vendor does not have available at the time of the contract (future goods) passes when, being in a deliverable state, they are allocated to the buyer with his approval.

3. Title to goods that are sold by reference to type only, no specific individual units being identified (unascertained goods) passes as under item 2 above.

4. Title to specific goods ('I want that one there') passes when the contract is made, if the goods are in a deliverable state, or, where the goods are not in a deliverable state or need to be measured, weighed or tested, when the buyer has been notified that whatever was necessary has been done.

5. Title to goods sold on approval or sale or return passes when the buyer accepts them (see 'Have the goods been accepted?' below).

6. Title to goods sold by someone not the legal owner and acting without authority remains with the legal owner, except that an innocent buyer obtains good title if the owner knows of the transaction and does not intervene (estoppel); he buys in a shop in the City of London or in certain markets, openly and from a dealer in that type of goods, and no one has been convicted of their theft (market overt); as a private person and not a dealer he buys a vehicle subject to hire purchase; he buys from a factor goods belonging to his principal; the seller has only a voidable title, but action to rescind has not been taken by the original owner at the time of the sale (see 'Is the contract voidable?', pp. 101–3); or he buys and takes possession of goods which the vendor has already contracted to sell to someone else.

Have the goods been accepted?
Acceptance of goods may be either stated, or implied by the buyer's behaviour or by retention of the goods beyond a specified time – as with goods on approval – or beyond a reasonable time if none is specified.

Under the Misrepresentation Act 1967 a buyer cannot be deemed to have accepted goods until he has had a reasonable opportunity to examine them, albeit it might otherwise be inferred from his behaviour that he had accepted them.

Remedies for Breach, Misrepresentation and Frustration

Any of the following remedies either individually or in combination may, in the right circumstances, be employed by or against you.

REMEDIES AGAINST GOODS   *problem 69*
1. Where the buyer becomes insolvent an unpaid seller may retain the goods if they are still in his possession or stop the goods in transit and regain possession if he has reserved this right. The seller will then have to await payment and may only resell the goods if they are perishable or if he gives notice of his intention and the buyer does not then pay within a reasonable time.

2. Where the buyer is solvent an unpaid seller may retain the goods only if they are still in his possession and either they were not sold on credit or a period of credit granted has expired. He must then await payment or resell the goods as in item 1 above.

3. For a buyer's right against goods which he has contracted to purchase but of which he is denied possession see 'Specific performance', p. 110.

REJECTION OF GOODS   *problem 70*
Provided they have not already been accepted (see 'Disputes over title to goods' above) goods may be rejected if they have not been delivered in accordance with the terms of the contract.

EXAMPLE: X orders 100 dresses but receives only eighty. He may now reject the delivery or retain the eighty, for which he must pay.

Rejection of goods for a valid reason does not necessarily result in the discharge of the contract.

Where a buyer wrongfully refuses to accept goods for which he has contracted the seller will have a right to damages.

DISCHARGE   *problem 71*

The innocent party may consider himself discharged from his obligations under a contract (and may in addition be entitled to other remedies) where:

1. His offer to perform his part of the contract is refused.

2. The other party does not perform his part in time (see 'Has the contract been performed in time?' above).

3. It is definite that the other party has no intention of performing his part (anticipatory breach).

4. There has been a total failure by the other party to perform his part.

5. There has been misrepresentation (see pp. 101–2 and 111).

6. There has been a breach of condition, that is, of something vital to the contract.

EXAMPLE: *Poussard* v. *Spiers* (1876). Because of illness an actress was not able to perform in an operetta until a week after it had opened. It was held that there had been a breach of condition and the producers could repudiate.

But where partial performance is accepted, then reasonable payment must be made.

The innocent party is not discharged where the breach is of a warranty, that is, of something not vital to the main purpose of the contract (and therefore the remedy is damages).

EXAMPLE: *Bettini* v. *Gye* (1876). An opera singer arrived in time for only three days' rehearsal instead of six. It was held that there had been a breach of warranty only and the contract could not be repudiated.

Both parties to a contract may be discharged from their obligations by agreement or by frustration (see 'Has the contract been frustrated?' pp. 104–5 and 'Frustration', p. 111).

SUING FOR PAYMENT   *problem 71*

1. An unpaid seller may sue for the price of goods that have been accepted by the other party.

2. Where a buyer wrongfully rejects goods the remedy is damages.

3. Where partial performance has been accepted reasonable payment must be made.

108

BUT: *Sumpter* v. *Hedges* (1898). Sumpter abandoned his contract to build two houses for Hedges after doing only part of the work. It was held that Sumpter was not entitled to any payment because Hedges had been given no choice but to accept the work Sumpter had already done. (The circumstances here are unusual; building agreements normally provide for payments at various stages of the work.)

4. Where performance is substantial then full payment must be made less allowance for the breaches of warranty.

EXAMPLE: *Dakin* v. *Lee* (1916). It was held that where builders Dakin & Co had contracted to repair Mrs Lee's house for £264 and there were defects in the work, they were entitled to the contract sum less an allowance for the defects.

Quantum meruit

An injured party in a breach of contract may claim *quantum meruit*, meaning 'as much as he has earned'.

EXAMPLE: *Planché* v. *Colburn* (1831). Colburn engaged Planché to write on ancient armour for the Juvenile Library for a fee of £100. The publication folded before Planché had completed his treatise and he sued for the work he had done and recovered £50.

DAMAGES   *problems 72–74*

The basic remedy for breach of contract is damages and it may be applied on its own or in conjunction with other remedies. Damages are either nominal or substantial, and liquidated or unliquidated.

Nominal

Nominal damages are merely a token award where the plaintiff has had his case upheld by the court but no actual loss has resulted from the breach.

Substantial

Substantial damages seek to reinstate the plaintiff in the financial position that he would have been in if the breach had not occurred. The plaintiff must mitigate his loss.

EXAMPLE: H—— Mc—— ordered £2,000 worth of vinyl sheeting but upon delivery returned it to the manufacturers because he had changed his mind. The manufacturers could not sue for £2,000 because they had the sheeting which they could sell elsewhere.

Liquidated
Where a contract specifies the amount of damages payable in the event of a breach and they are a *genuine pre-estimate*, then they are 'liquidated' damages and the court will award them.

Unliquidated
Where a contract specifies no amount payable as damages in the event of a breach and the court makes its own assessment, then these are 'unliquidated' damages. The court may substitute unliquidated damages for 'penal' damages – that is, damages specified in a contract that are not a genuine pre-estimate but are by way of threat.

SPECIFIC PERFORMANCE   *problem 75*
The court will only order specific performance, – that is, order the defendant to fulfil his part of the contract – where:

1. Damages are unable to compensate the plaintiff.

EXAMPLE: X contracts to buy a unique work of art but the vendor later changes his mind and refuses to sell. Damages would not enable X to purchase a similar piece.

2. In addition to item 1 above, court supervision of performance is practical. The court will never order specific performance of a contract for personal service, and cannot where goods have been resold by the seller.

Damages may be awarded in addition to specific performance.

PROHIBITORY INJUNCTION
A prohibitory injunction orders a defendant not to do something.

EXAMPLE: *Warner Bros* v. *Nelson* (1937). An actress contracted to act exclusively for Warner Bros for one year but broke her contract. Warner Bros could not obtain an order for specific performance compelling the actress to work for them but they did obtain a prohibitory injunction preventing her from working for anyone else. The actress was also liable for damages.

110

Misrepresentation

The injured party may refuse to perform his part of the contract; ask the court to rescind the contract, restoring both parties to their pre-contract positions; claim damages; or claim damages for fraud where the misrepresentation was fraudulent.

Rescission is not available where the innocent party has had benefit or where goods have been processed or sold to an innocent third party.

Frustration

Both parties are restored to their pre-contract position, allowance being made for expenses incurred and valuable benefit received.

EXAMPLE: *Fibrosa* v. *Fairburn* (1943). Fibrosa, a Polish company, ordered £4,800 worth of machinery, paying £1,000 in advance. The German invasion of Poland frustrated the contract and Fibrosa were held entitled to recover their £1,000.

PROBLEMS AND SOLUTIONS

Justice is frequently dispensed slowly, sometimes not at all, and either way it costs a good deal. Since all the time it is growing more difficult to obtain justice inside a court, so consequently it is becoming harder to obtain justice outside of it. The guilty party may force the innocent to accept an unjust settlement out of court by reason of the triple obstacles above that the innocent will otherwise have to contend with.

No matter how carefully you prepare your contracts they will not of themselves compel anyone to do anything; you cannot beat or shoot anybody with them. You must so construct your affairs, as far as is possible, that the remedy for breach lies in your own hands, putting the onus on the other party to initiate action in the courts if he is not satisfied. For example, you engage a contractor to repair a leaking factory roof and the leaks continue. You decline to pay the contract price. If the tiler is not satisfied (you may have decided to pay him nothing), then he can go to court. Where faults are not likely to be immediately apparent you should delay payment until time has made its test. On the other hand, if you are the contractor, you should request payment in advance. Again, a businessman buys a company. If he is wise he retains part of the purchase price against misrepresentation; if the vendors are wise they will not allow him to do so.

53. I supplied goods to a wholesaler making it a condition that he dealt only with small accounts and left the larger retailers for me to deal with direct. Now I find he has supplied a store close to an existing substantial customer of mine and they are very upset about it.

You have no remedy against the store as they made no contract with you. You may have a remedy against the wholesaler in damages, if your existing customer cancels orders. You may be able to consider your obligation to supply further quantities to the wholesaler under the contract discharged, if this breach is fundamental to the contract. Reassure your customer that this will not happen again and, if necessary, consider buying up the merchandise in the other store.

54. A property dealer paid me £5 for an option to buy land at the rear of my factory. No price was agreed at the time. The option does not expire for six months but I have now had a definite offer for the land from someone else and would like to accept.

As no price for the land was agreed, then, in the absence of any formula for arriving at a price being contained in the option, the option is not valid. There is no offer in law; you cannot agree to agree.

55. I owe £10,000 to a bank under a personal guarantee but they have agreed to accept £2,000 in full and final settlement. I want to make sure that this is binding before I pay.

It will not be as the bank is receiving no consideration for its promise to accept less than it is already entitled to. It will be if you arrange for a third party to pay with their consent. (Also where the lesser sum is paid before the full amount is due or where it is paid in a different place or where it is under a composition in settlement in bankruptcy.)

56. When I sold my business I agreed never to enter into the same line of business again. I now realise that this was rather rash; I need to earn my living again and it is the only trade I know.

Restraints of this kind are void unless it can be shown that they are reasonable, not more than is required and not against public interest. On the face of it this restraint looks void. But if your returning to the same line of business would have a serious impact on your old firm, then it may be that the restraint is valid. In this case consider buying out the restraint.

57. I have a ten years' solus agreement with a petrol company to sell only their products at my garage and I want to get out of it.
Generally, five years is considered the maximum for this type of restraint, so you may be able to.

58. An outlet is selling my products at a loss to attract business and this has disrupted trade with my other customers.
The Resale Prices Act 1964 permits the withholding of supplies where products are used as 'loss-leaders'.

59. I have been selling certain products at a very keen price. Now I am having difficulty obtaining supplies and I suspect that this is because the manufacturers do not like what I am doing.
Under the Resale Prices Act 1964 the withholding of supplies in an attempt to fix a minimum price is illegal.

60. My bank manager produced a guarantee for me to sign and I did so without reading it or understanding what I was doing. Now they are suing me for payment under it.
The contract will not be void unless you were led to believe that it was not a guarantee that you were signing or unless you were obviously drunk or otherwise mentally incapable of understanding what you were doing.

61. I have brought an action for breach. The defendant claims that the contract does not express what was agreed.
He will have to prove quite conclusively that the written contract differs from the terms agreed orally beforehand. It will be hard enough to prove if it is true, let alone if it is not.

62. I have discovered some errors in a contract, including misspellings of names. Will this make it invalid?
If they are obvious – no.

63. I have lent £10,000 to a private company. I am now informed that the company has exceeded its borrowing powers and that I can neither claim interest nor recover the money.

Under the European Communities Act 1972 you can do both, provided you were not aware that the company was acting *ultra vires*.

64. I run my own small travel business and get a lot of business from students and other young people under the age of eighteen who book holidays, cancel, then demand their deposit back.

A minor cannot be sued for the price of goods or services that are mere luxuries unnecessary to maintain him in his station in life. Furthermore, a minor will be able to recover any money paid on a contract for 'unnecessaries' if he has received no benefit. A holiday would probably be considered as 'unnecessary' and therefore you will not be able to retain a deposit or obtain satisfaction over cancellations. The solution is to obtain an indemnity from an adult.

65. I entered into a contract on the strength of what I consider to have been misleading information; the other party says 'let the buyer beware'.

Misrepresentations are untrue statements of fact made by the other party to the contract, outside and prior to the contract and by which you were influenced. Possible remedies if you have suffered loss are rescission and damages, or you may be able to refuse to perform your part of the contract (see 'Remedies', pp. 107–11). *Caveat emptor* – let the buyer beware – allows a person to keep silent over defects (unless asked) but not to make misrepresentations.

66. My company borrowed from a bank. After a year the bank said they would only renew the facility if I gave my house as security. I was forced to agree because the business would have collapsed otherwise. Now I wonder if this amounts to duress or undue influence.

No. But see Chapter One, II.

67. I have exchanged contracts to buy a piece of land but a

hitch has developed over finance. Completion date is in one week.

Time is not 'of the essence' in contracts for the sale of land unless they specifically state otherwise. If you do not complete on the contract date you will receive a notice requiring you to complete within a certain period as laid down in the contract, usually twenty-one days. So you probably have a month before you stand to forfeit your deposit and, in addition, become liable to damages. This should give you time to iron out your arrangements or possibly negotiate with someone else for them to take over and complete.

68. At an antiques fair I offered £200 for a Victorian microscope, which was accepted, and gave the stallholder my card saying I would be back at the end of the day to settle up. When I went back the microscope was gone, and the dealer said it had been stolen.

As you were the legal owner, then you suffer the loss. But as you have not paid, keep your money on the grounds that it was implicit that the vendor would keep the microscope safe and that he had been negligent and hope that the case does not come to court. If the dealer had sold the microscope to someone else, having been offered a better price, this would be a case of the seller reselling and the second purchaser would obtain good title. Your remedy would be damages for loss of profit.

69. I have just found out that a company to whom I have sent goods by train is unable to meet its commitments as they fall due. The goods are still at the station, at the other end.

Goods in transit to a buyer who cannot meet bills as they fall due may be taken back to await payment if that right has been reserved; but these goods are no longer in transit as the carrier is holding them for the purchaser. In practical terms, what is the company likely to do if you manage to get the goods back? Taking another approach, it is an offence for a director of a limited company to order goods knowing the company to be insolvent, and you might be able to use this as a weapon.

70. Goods were delivered four weeks ago and I have not yet paid for them. I have just discovered a fault.

It seems likely that after four weeks you will be deemed to have accepted the goods in which case you will not now be able to reject the goods and the remedy is damages. But since you have not paid, then from the practical point of view you should either send the goods back and see what the vendors do or reduce the payment to take account of the damages.

71. My decorating firm commenced work on a factory but at the end of the first day the managing director said he was not happy with the way my firm was tackling the job and told us not to come back.
A contract can only be discharged by breach if it is of something vital and fundamental. You may have a claim for payment for work done and for damages.

72. A clause in a contract awards a penalty of £500 for every week that delivery by us is late. It is late.
If £500 was a genuine pre-estimate of the actual weekly loss through late delivery, then the court will award it. If not, and the £500 was by way of threat, then the court will award damages related to the actual loss.

73. My company inserted a clause into a contract with a supplier that the contract price would be reduced by £200 for every week that delivery was delayed. Delivery is late but our losses are running at £500 a week.
If the £200 was a genuine pre-estimate at the time the contract was made and was not merely by way of threat, then it is valid and you cannot recover your true losses. These clauses are of little value. If the pre-estimate is too high it will be seen as a penalty and be invalid; if too low, as in this case, you lose.

74. I contracted to make a component but was unable to deliver on time. The buyer has now told me that the component was vital and that he is going to sue me for loss of profits while his factory is shut down.
Harm must be foreseeable at the time a contract is made. If you were not aware of the consequences of late delivery on the factory when you made the contract, you cannot be held liable for those consequences now.

75. I agreed to sell a valuable antique but have now changed my mind and intend to keep it. The other party says he can get an order compelling me to give it up.

Specific performance might be awarded in this case as the goods are presumably unique, but not if you had meanwhile resold them to a third party, who would get good title, in which case the purchaser's remedy would be damages only.

USEFUL BOOKS

Anson, Sir W. R. (ed. A. G. Guest), *Law of Contract* (OUP, 1975)

Furmston, M. P. (ed.), *Chesire & Fifoot's Law of Contract* (Butterworth, 1976)

Greig, D. W., *Sale of Goods* (Butterworth, 1974)

6

THE LAW FOR EMPLOYERS

In which we consider an employer's responsibility for employees' acts; the terms and conditions of employment; health and safety; discrimination; trade unions and industrial relations: short-time, lay-off, dismissal and redundancy; and the position with regard to independent contractors and agents.

Businessmen report that, after financing problems, the responsibilities of being an employer are the next big cause of ulcers. The employer can do a lot to relieve his problems by familiarising himself with all the details of employment legislation and conforming to the often trivial requirements that are nevertheless a source of friction with employees. Insurance can soothe some ulcers.

Legislation on employment matters is both massive and continual. Below are set out what are considered to be the important points for the smaller businessman at the date of writing. The employer is advised to obtain copies of the relevant Acts or of the explanatory booklets issued by the Department of Employment etc.

A person is an employee if he has either an oral or written contract of service or a contract that gives details of wages, hours, holidays, pension rights etc. A person is probably an employee if his employer makes a National Insurance contribution on his behalf or he works under direct control.

Employer's Responsibility for Employees' Acts *problems 76, 77*

An employer is liable whenever an employee commits a tort (a wrong) in the course of his employment.

Century Insurance Co Ltd v. *Northern Ireland Road Transport Board* (1942). It was held that his employers were liable for a fire caused when a petrol tanker driver lit a cigarette while filling an underground tank at a garage. The driver was carrying out an authorised task.

London County Council v. *Cattermoles (Garages) Ltd* (1953). It was held that his employers were liable when a garage hand, who was employed to move vehicles in a garage by pushing them, drove a van and caused an accident, although his employers had forbidden him to drive vehicles. Again, he was carrying out an authorised task, albeit in an unauthorised manner.

Poland v. *Parr* (1927). An employee on his way home struck a boy who he believed was stealing sugar from his employers' lorry. The boy fell and had to have a leg amputated. The man's employers were held liable. Although the man was not employed to guard the sugar, an employee has a duty to take reasonable steps to protect his employer's property.

BUT: *Ricketts* v. *Thos. Tilling Ltd* (1915). It was held that his employers were not liable when a bus conductor drove a bus and injured someone. He was not carrying out work that he was authorised to do, nor was he acting within implied authority or to further a proper objective of his employer. However, his employer was still held liable for the negligence of the bus driver in allowing the conductor to move the bus.

An employee is also himself liable for his own torts but it is inevitably the employer who is sued. An employee has a common law duty to compensate his employer for losses suffered as a result of his, the employee's, torts.

Terms and Conditions of Employment   *problems 78–85*

The Wages Councils Act 1959; Employment Protection Act 1975; Employment Protection (Consolidation) Act 1978; Common Law.

Employees must be given *written statements* of the terms of their employment within thirteen weeks of starting work (and the statements must be kept up to date), unless they have contracts of service which contain the necessary details and which are kept up to date.

Employees must also be given *itemised pay statements*. Employers are exempt from these requirements in respect of certain categories of employee, and the exceptions that are of most significance for the small businessman are:

1. Employees who normally work less than sixteen hours a week (but those who have worked from eight to sixteen hours a week for five years will still need a statement). A person who normally works sixteen hours or more a week but then drops to between eight and sixteen hours will be covered by the requirements for a period of twenty-six weeks.

2. An employee who is the husband or wife of the employer.

The statement of employment terms must include the following (or, where appropriate, should refer the employee to other notices or documents):

1. Names of employer and employee.

2. Date employment began and, where service with a previous employer can be taken into account for the calculation of redundancy pay, for example where there has been a change of ownership of the business, the date the continuous service began.

3. The rate of remuneration or method of calculating it, the intervals at which it will be paid and the hours of work.

4. Details of holiday entitlement, holiday pay, sick pay and pension scheme.

5. The period of notice the employee has to give and is entitled to receive.

6. Job title.

7. Details of disciplinary rules.

8. The name or title of a person to whom the employee may complain if he has a grievance or to whom he may appeal against a disciplinary decision, and the procedure for so doing.

9. The expiry date if a fixed-term contract.

The itemised pay statement must show the gross amount of wages or salary; any variable and fixed deductions; the net amount payable; and the methods of payment where the payment is split.

An employee who considers that these requirements are not being met may apply to an industrial tribunal.

REMUNERATION

1. An employer must meet wages council minimum requirements on rates of pay, hours, holidays etc, if applicable to his workers. Failure to comply lays the employer open to a fine on each offence and an order compelling him to pay compensation

to his employees for the wages they should have received during the preceding two years.

2. An employer must meet the 'recognised terms and conditions' as agreed between employers' associations and independent trade unions representing a substantial proportion of employers and employees. If he does not do so then a trade union concerned may report the matter to the Advisory, Conciliation and Arbitration Service (ACAS). An employer must also meet the 'general level of terms and conditions' for a particular type of employee that prevail in similar companies in the same area in the same trade. If he does not do so, then the trade union of an employee affected may report the matter to ACAS (except that a recognised union must make the report if the employer already recognises a different union for that type of employee). In these cases if ACAS cannot reach an agreement by conciliation then the Central Arbitration Committee (CAC) may make an award such that the terms and conditions become an implied term of the contract of employment. (This procedure is not available where terms and conditions or the mechanism for settling them come under other legislation. But the procedure is available where employees are also covered by wages councils.)

3. An employer must pay both piece and time workers under common law even if no work is available unless he has the right to lay them off or put them on short-time or the cause of there being no work is beyond his control.

TIME OFF

Employees who are officials of trade unions recognised by their employers are entitled to reasonable time off with pay to carry out their duties. Employers must also allow reasonable time off to trade union members to allow them to take part in trade union activities and to employees who have public duties (justices of the peace, members of local authorities etc).

A pregnant woman is entitled to leave work eleven weeks before her confinement and claim six weeks' *maternity pay* (which her employer may recover from the Maternity Pay Fund), provided she has two years' continuous service at that point. She may claim the right to return to work at any time up to twenty-nine weeks after the week of her confinement.

NOTICE

An employer must give at least one week's notice to an employee who has worked for him for more than four weeks but less than two years, and after an employee has been with him for two or more years the employer must give at least one week's notice for each year of employment (maximum twelve). If he does not the employee may seek damages. No notice has to be given to or by a person employed on a fixed-term contract of less than twelve weeks or on a job expected to last, and which does last, less than twelve weeks. An employee must give at least one week's notice after four weeks' service.

JOB TITLE

An employee may refuse to perform work that does not come under his job title and that does not form part of the duties of the job or that was not specified in the statement or contract.

DISCIPLINE

The common law duties of an employee are to obey proper instructions (but see 'Job title' above); to exercise care and skill; to compensate his employer for losses resulting from his own wrongdoing (he must at the same time be indemnified by his employer against liabilities incurred on his employer's behalf); not to be rude, lazy, dishonest, drunk or immoral; and not to make secret profits, pass on trade secrets, take bribes or keep for himself products developed with his employer's facilities. (See also 'Health and safety' below.)

Health and Safety   *problems 86–88*

Employer's Liability (Defective Equipment) Act 1969; Health and Safety at Work Act 1974 (replacing Factories Act 1961); Social Security Act 1975; Employment Protection (Consolidation) Act 1978; Common Law.

Employers must:

1. Take all reasonable precautions to ensure the safety of employees and visitors to their premises.

2. Provide safe plant and premises, a safe system of work and competent fellow employees.

3. Use the best practicable means of preventing harmful emissions into the atmosphere.

4. Provide a written statement of safety policy and allow trade unions to appoint safety representatives for consultation.

5. Meet the legally enforceable regulations issued by the Secretary of State from time to time and observe the codes of practice issued by the Health and Safety Commission.

6. Obey notices issued by factory inspectors. Inspectors have the power to issue improvement notices requiring work to be carried out within a reasonable time to correct a breach of regulations, but which are suspended pending an appeal to an industrial tribunal; and prohibition notices ordering a shutdown, and which are not suspended pending an appeal to an industrial tribunal.

EXAMPLES:

Vaughan v. *Roper & Co Ltd* (1947). It was held that shipowners were liable for their failure to supply sufficient spare rope. The plant was inadequate.

Donnelly v. *Glasgow Corporation* (1953). It was held that the defendants were liable when a bus overturned because of a broken spring and the driver was injured.

Speed v. *Thomas Swift & Co Ltd* (1943). Speed was loading a ship from a barge. The hook caught in a rail which fell and injured him. It was held that his employers were liable as they had failed to set out a safe system of work.

Clifford v. *Charles M. Challen & Son Ltd* (1951). It was held that his employers were liable when a workman contracted dermatitis, even though a protective cream had been provided. The foreman had been slack in promoting its use.

BUT: *Woods* v. *Durable Suites Ltd* (1953). It was held that his employers were not liable when an employee contracted dermatitis, because they had done everything reasonable to ensure that the protective cream provided was used.

Latimer v. *AEC* (1952). It was held that his employers were not liable when an employee slipped on a floor that had been flooded as they had done everything reasonable to dry it out.

Burns v. *Joseph Terry & Sons Ltd* (1951). A cocoa-grinding machine was properly fenced, but not from above. Burns climbed a ladder to clear the machine and was injured. It was held that his employers were not liable as it could not have been foreseen that anyone would do this.

BUT: *John Summers & Sons Ltd* v. *Frost* (1955). It was held that where an employee was injured by a grindstone the impracticability of fixing a guard was not a defence.

HOWEVER: *Nicholls* v. *F. Austin (Leyton) Ltd* (1946). It was held that an employer was not liable for broken parts ejected from a machine causing injury (unless by failure to maintain the machine properly).

An employee must take reasonable care for the health and safety of himself and of other persons who may be affected by his acts or omissions at work.

MEDICAL SUSPENSION

An employee with at least four weeks' continuous service who is capable of work but because of statutory requirements or recommendations under the Health and Safety at Work Act 1974 is suspended on medical grounds is entitled to up to twenty-six weeks' pay from his employer. The employer can offer suitable alternative work instead.

INSURANCE

Employers must take out employers' liability and public liability insurance to cover themselves in the event of claims for damages. Employees are insured against personal injury or disease arising out of and in the course of employment under the Social Security Act 1975.

Discrimination

Equal Pay Act 1970; Rehabilitation of Offenders Act 1974; Sex Discrimination Act 1975; Race Relations Act 1976; Employment Protection (Consolidation) Act 1978.

An employer may not discriminate on grounds of the following:

1. Sex. Men and women working for the same employer or group of companies must have equal pay and conditions for doing the same or equal work, except as provided by statute (for example, for pregnancy) or where there is a differential for higher production or length of service etc. It is unlawful to refuse to employ on grounds of sex except where the job essentially requires a particular sex, as in the case of a model, a lavatory attendant, a masseuse etc.

2. Marital status. It is unlawful to discriminate in employment against a person because he or she is married.

3. Convictions. A person whose conviction is spent – that is, he has not had a further conviction for a specified period – may not

be discriminated against on account of his past convictions. (There are exceptions for certain types of offence and for certain types of employer.)

4. Colour, race, nationality, or ethnic or national origins. But an employer may seek employees of a particular racial group where that is a genuine occupational qualification. The Race Relations Act 1976 admits four categories – authenticity in entertainment, authenticity in modelling, work in a restaurant and welfare work among a particular racial group. 'Positive' discrimination is allowed in training for work in which a particular racial group is under-represented.

5. Trade union membership. An employer may not discriminate on the grounds that a person is a member of an independent trade union (except where it is the wrong union under a closed-shop agreement).

6. Pregnancy. An employer may not dismiss a woman simply because she is pregnant. (See 'Dismissal', pp. 126–8.)

Trade Unions and Industrial Relations *problems 89–92*

Trade Union and Labour Relations Act 1974; Employment Protection Act 1975; Trade Union and Labour Relations (Amendment) Act 1976.

1. An employee has the right to join and take part in the activities of an independent trade union and to have time off as discussed on p. 121.

2. It is lawful to picket in furtherance of a trade dispute in order peacefully to obtain or communicate information, or peacefully to persuade at a place where a person works or happens to be (though not his home).

3. A collective agreement is not legally enforceable unless it is in writing and contains a clause to that effect; nor can a court compel an employee to work or attend work.

ADVISORY, CONCILIATION AND ARBITRATION SERVICE
ACAS was set up by the Employment Protection Act 1975 to give advice to employers and trade unions; to conciliate on disputes over dismissal, redundancy, terms of employment etc; to arrange arbitration if so requested by both parties; and to consider recognition disputes, where an employer refuses to recognise a union for collective bargaining.

Union recognition

An independent union that has been denied recognition by an employer may refer the dispute to ACAS. If ACAS cannot achieve a settlement by conciliation, then after an investigation into the wishes of employees it may (or may not) recommend recognition. An employer may appeal. If he does not appeal or his appeal is rejected and he still refuses union recognition, then ACAS will again try to conciliate. Failure means that the union may apply to the Central Arbitration Committee, which may impose the terms and conditions of employment claimed by the trade union or such other terms and conditions as it considers appropriate.

If the employer still refuses to recognise the union or to observe any of the other terms and conditions awarded by the CAC, then the union may take action in the courts.

Short-time, Lay-off, Dismissal and Redundancy

Redundancy Payments Act 1965; Trade Union and Labour Relations Act 1974 and Amendment Act 1976; Employment Protection Act 1975; Employment Protection (Consolidation) Act 1978; Common Law.

LAY-OFF AND SHORT-TIME   *problem 93*

If laid off for a whole day (but not because of a dispute involving other employees of the same or an associated employer), an employee with at least four weeks' continuous service will be entitled to a guarantee payment. This is equal to the hourly rate multiplied by normal hours worked daily with a limit of £6.60 and is paid for up to the number of days in a three-month period commencing on the first of February, May, August or November that an employee normally works in one week (maximum five).

An employer is entitled to offer other suitable work and will not have to make a guarantee payment if the employee refuses it.

If an employee does not receive a guarantee payment to which he is entitled, he may complain to an industrial tribunal.

Continued lay-off or short-time may entitle an employee to claim for redundancy and leave his employment (see below).

DISMISSAL   *problems 94–99*

An employee is dismissed:

126

1. If his employer terminates his contract of employment with or without notice.

2. If he leaves his employment with or without notice because his employer's conduct entitles him to.

3. If he is on a fixed-term contract which is not renewed upon its expiry.

When is dismissal unfair?
'Unfair' is a term introduced by statute. The easiest way to define it is to say that dismissal is unfair whenever it cannot be shown to be fair. In particular it is unfair if:

1. It is for trade union membership or activities.

2. It is for refusal to join a non-independent trade union (a trade union under domination or control or strong influence of the employer).

3. Re-engagement is not offered after a lock-out.

4. It is because an employee is pregnant, unless she has become incapable of doing her work and there is no other suitable vacancy.

5. A woman who has given proper notice of her intention to return to work is not permitted to return to her old job or, where there has been redundancy, to a suitable alternative position, within the twenty-nine-week period following the week of her confinement.

When is dismissal fair?
Dismissal *may* be fair if it is because:

1. The employee does not have the capability or qualifications for the work he was employed to do.

2. Of misconduct.

3. The employee is redundant.

4. A statute would otherwise be contravened.

5. The employee was taken on as a temporary replacement, and knew this, and the person he is replacing returns to work.

Dismissal is not automatically fair in any of the above circumstances. The employer must act reasonably, having regard to all the circumstances.

Dismissal is automatically fair if it is because an employee is not or refuses to become a member of a specified independent trade union under a closed-shop agreement (unless refusal is on religious grounds or he is a member of another union which has referred a recognition claim to ACAS).

When is dismissal wrongful?

Dismissal is 'wrongful' under common law if proper notice is not given; an employee is summarily dismissed without just cause; or an employee is dismissed during a fixed-term contract without just cause.

Employee's action when dismissal is unfair or wrongful

Employees have the right not to be unfairly dismissed. An employee who considers that his dismissal was unfair may complain to an industrial tribunal within three months of dismissal. If they agree they may order reinstatement (as if the employee had never been dismissed), re-engagement or compensation. An employee may be entitled to a further special compensatory award if an employer refuses a tribunal's recommendation for reinstatement or re-engagement.

Certain employees may not complain of unfair dismissal unless it is for an 'inadmissible reason', that is, connected with trade union membership. These exceptions are part-time employees working less than sixteen hours a week (eight hours if they have been so employed for five years); employees with less than twenty-six weeks' continuous service; and employees who have reached normal retirement age in their job. Amongst those employees who may not complain at all are the husband or wife of the employer and those whose fixed-term contracts made prior to 28 February 1972 expired and were not renewed. An employee may agree in a fixed-term contract of two or more years not to claim unfair dismissal on its expiry if it is not renewed.

An employee who has been wrongfully dismissed may take action in the courts.

Statement of reasons for dismissal

An employee with twenty-six weeks' service has a right to request and be given a written statement of the reasons for his dismissal. An industrial tribunal will award two weeks' pay for refusal to comply.

An employer will not be liable for defamatory statements unless made maliciously.

References   *problems 100, 101*

An employer is not obliged to provide references.

An employer who makes a redundancy payment under the Redundancy Payments Act 1965 may claim a rebate of (at the time of writing) 41 per cent from the Redundancy Fund.

A redundancy payment is calculated as follows, reckonable service being limited to a maximum of twenty years and reckonable pay to a maximum of £100 a week.

1. One-and-a-half weeks' pay for each year of reckonable service from age 41 to age 65 (man) and 60 (woman).

2. One week's pay for each year of reckonable service from age 22 to age 40.

3. Half a week's pay for each year of reckonable service from age 18 to age 21.

The maximum payment is therefore £3,000.

The payment is reduced by one-twelfth for each complete month a man is over 64 or a woman over 59 when the contract terminates.

Who is redundant?

An employee is redundant if he is dismissed wholly or mainly because his employer no longer needs so many employees of his particular type at the address at which the employee has contracted to work. See above for the definition of dismissal.

An employee may consider himself 'redundant' if he has been laid off or on short-time or a mixture of both either for four consecutive weeks or for a total of six weeks in a thirteen-week period. (A week of lay-off is one in which an employee gets no pay; a week of short-time is one in which an employee gets less than half-pay.) He must then serve notice on his employer within four weeks of the last day of a period of continuous lay-off or short-time or a thirteen-week period which contained six weeks of lay-off or short-time, saying that he intends to claim a redundancy payment. His employer may serve a counter-notice within seven days denying liability on the grounds that normal working will be resumed within four weeks and continue for at least thirteen weeks. Contested cases will be decided by an industrial tribunal; in non-contested cases the employee, having given notice to leave his employment, must leave on its expiry when his redundancy pay will become due.

Which redundant employees are entitled to redundancy pay?

An employee who is redundant is generally entitled to redundancy pay if he has worked 104 weeks without a break in continuity with the same employer for a minimum of sixteen hours a week (eight hours if continuously employed for five years or more) and is at least 20 years of age.

However, in certain circumstances, such a redundant employee has no entitlement. For the small businessman the most significant exclusions are the employee who:

1. Is 65 when his reckonable service ends (60 if a woman).

2. Is the wife (or husband) of the employer.

3. Entered into a two-year or longer fixed-term contract after the passing of the Redundancy Payments Act 1965 in which he agreed to forego redundancy pay on its expiry. (But such an employee will still be entitled to redundancy pay if made redundant before the contract expires.)

Offer of further employment

A redundant employee is not entitled to redundancy pay if he *unreasonably* rejects an offer of further employment on the same terms as before or an offer of suitable alternative employment on different terms or at a different place with the same employer, with an associated employer or with the new owner of the business, provided that the offer is made before the expiry of his notice and the job starts not later than four weeks after the end of the current contract.

An employee who accepts alternative employment as above is entitled to a four-week trial period during which the redundancy payment he would have had becomes due if he gives notice for any reason or is given notice because he is considered unsuitable for the job.

Trade union consultation

An employer who recognises an independent trade union for the category to which a redundant employee belongs must consult with that trade union before dismissal whether the employee is a member or not. Failure to do so may result in enforcement of a protective award by an industrial tribunal giving the employee the right to a normal week's pay, whether he is still working or not, for up to twenty-eight days (sixty days if he is one of ten or more redundant employees, ninety days if he is one of 100 or more).

Employees covered by collective agreements on redundancies who have been excluded by the Secretary of State for Employment are not covered by this provision, nor are employees for a fixed term of twelve weeks or less who do not work any longer.

Notification to Department of Employment
Employers must notify the Secretary of State for Employment where ten or more employees are to be made redundant over a short period, or risk reduction of rebate.

Independent Contractors

Vicarious liability   *problem 107*
An employer is not usually liable for the wrongful acts of independent contractors unless he has been negligent by engaging someone incompetent; he has given negligent instructions; he has engaged them to carry out work which causes subsidence to neighbouring property or which constitutes a danger to users of the highway or which causes dust and noise; or the contractor works as a part of his organisation and a person entrusts himself to the organisation as a whole – as, for example, where a consultant performs an operation at a hospital.

Safety
An employer must take all reasonable steps to ensure the safety of people at work in his premises, including independent contractors.

Breach of contract
See Chapter Five.

Discrimination
As for contracts of service (see pp. 124–5).

Redundancy and dismissal
Someone engaged under a contract for services cannot be entitled to redundancy pay, nor can a self-employed person receive it. A sub-contractor cannot claim 'unfair' dismissal.

Commission Agents   *problems 108–110*

In legal terms a person who arranges a contract between a prin-

131

cipal and a third party is an agent. Thus, the managing director of a company is an agent. These notes are not concerned with agency in its wide legal sense but only with commission agency in the narrow commercial sense.

CREATION
Creation may be:

1. Express, by deed or written or oral contract. A principal is strongly advised to use a written contract and in particular to clarify areas likely to cause dispute – inability to deliver, termination of agency where orders are outstanding etc.

2. Implied, as regards third parties, by the behaviour of the principal.

3. By ratification of a contract made by someone who was not an agent of the principal but who passed himself off as such to the third party.

(Creation may also be by necessity.

EXAMPLE: *G. N. Railway* v. *Swaffield* (1874). It was held that the railway acted as agents of necessity when they arranged the stabling of a horse which the consignee failed to collect and were thus able to recover expenses. But there must be an emergency, the agent must be unable to contact the principal and there must be some sort of prior contractual relationship between the parties.)

VICARIOUS LIABILITY
Principals are liable for frauds and certain other torts committed by their agents, arising out of and in the course of their work for the principal. Thus, a principal would be responsible for fraudulent claims about his products made by his agent.

BUT: *Eggington* v. *Reader* (1936). It was held that his principal was not liable where a commission agent for ladies' clothing injured someone while driving his car in the course of his work.

DUTIES OF AGENTS
Agents must not make secret profits; reveal confidential information about the principal's affairs; or delegate to a sub-agent, unless it is a trade custom or by agreement. In general, agents have no liability on contracts to third parties unless they fail to reveal that they are agents, or it is by custom as, for example,

with stockbrokers. But if they exceed their authority and the principal does not ratify then the third party may sue the agent for breach of warranty.

BUT: *Watteau* v. *Fenwick* (1893). It was held that where the manager of a public house bought cigars without the owner's authority, the owner was nevertheless liable because the manager was acting within his apparent authority.

This is the rule of estoppel, that where a principal leads a third party to suppose that someone is an agent or that the agent has a certain authority, then the principal is prevented from denying it. It is particularly important where an agency has been terminated.

TERMINATION

Where an agency is terminated, third parties who were aware of the agency should be informed, otherwise the principal will continue to be bound to contracts negotiated by the ex-agent.

PROBLEMS AND SOLUTIONS

76. I recently employed a man to assist the lorry driver with loading and unloading. At a pick-up, while the driver was inside the factory, this man started the lorry and drove it through the factory fence. He is not covered by insurance and I am being sued for vicarious liability.

Provided that driving the lorry formed no part of this man's duties and the lorry driver was not negligent in allowing this man to get at the wheel, then the accident did not arise in the course of his employment and you are not liable.

77. I expressly forbade an employee to work up a ladder without securing tools in accordance with the methods laid down. He ignored my instructions and injured a passer-by when a hammer dropped.

Albeit your employee ignored your express instructions, you are unfortunately still liable. But, for what it is worth, you may have a claim against your employee.

78. Employees have written statements of terms of employment which refer them to notices for rates of remuneration etc. Pay has been increased and I updated the relevant notice

but certain employees have now complained that their statements were not updated.

Statements of the terms of employment do not themselves have to be updated as long as they refer to documents which employees may consult. It is then sufficient if employees' attention is drawn to the updated documents.

79. I engaged a woman as a machinist. She has not proved very adequate and I asked her instead to work a small press for fixing studs to garments, on the same terms as before. She refused.

An employee cannot be required to do work for which he has not contracted. If you require flexibility you should make this clear at the outset and in the statement of terms of employment. But if this woman is incompetent in the job for which she was employed you may be able to dismiss her.

80. An employee who is a salesman earns £40 a week basic plus commission on goods delivered amounting to a further £60 a week. I have received a very substantial and profitable order from abroad and will not be able to channel the same quantity of goods on to the home market via this salesman.

In common law you have a duty to ensure that your salesman is able to earn his commission. You may have to consider that he is redundant and rearrange your home sales methods, perhaps with a commission agent.

81. None of my employees are members of trade unions and I am not a member of any trade or employers' association. I have received a notice from a wages council laying down certain minimum requirements that I just cannot afford to meet.

If the terms and conditions of employment for your type of business are laid down by a wages council then it would be illegal to ignore them, even with the consent of your employees. You may have to think in terms of redundancies.

82. A small number of my employees are members of a trade union, although I do not recognise a union for collective bargaining. Their union has complained to ACAS that I pay less than other similar firms in this area and in this trade.

The union will have to establish the 'general' level of terms and conditions and ACAS will then consider whether or not you are observing them. The sort of arguments you may use are that the companies used for comparison are not in the same district or in the same trade; that the circumstances of your company are quite different from those of the companies used for comparison; or that although some of the terms and conditions are below the general level, employees are compensated by other terms and conditions above the general level. An award made by ACAS becomes part of the contract of employment.

83. A shop steward has begun to take more time off for his duties than I can afford.

ACAS issues a Code of Practice which you should consult.

84. A competitor just down the road is able to undercut and win a lot of the contracts that should come to us simply because he pays his employees less than agreed between the employers' association and the trade unions.

You may ask your employers' association to report to ACAS that your competitor is not observing the 'recognised terms and conditions'. If ACAS agree they will award his employees the recognised terms and conditions which he must observe.

85. A trade union has reported to ACAS that I pay my employees less than the recognised rates as agreed between the trade union and the employers' association. But in my view the trade union represents only a small proportion of employees in this trade and the employers' association only a small proportion of employers.

Then you must refute that the rates of pay claimed by the union are the 'recognised terms'.

86. I am being sued by an employee who fell and hurt himself while not wearing the safety-harness that I had specifically instructed him to wear.

You may have a successful defence of *volenti non fit injuria* – that is, that your employee knowingly accepted the risk of working without the harness.

87. I am being sued by an employee who injured himself

while operating a machine, although he deliberately ignored the correct safety procedures.

You may get the damages reduced by pleading contributory negligence.

88. One of my employees was injured using a brand-new tool which was faulty.

He has a claim on you for your failure to supply safe plant, but you have a claim against the manufacturer.

89. A trade union has, for collective bargaining, demanded information about my business and affairs that I am simply not prepared to divulge.

Under the Employment Protection Act 1975 an employer has a duty to disclose information without which 'trade union representatives would be to a material extent impeded in carrying on ... collective bargaining'. Therefore you must claim that the information requested is totally irrelevant. Other grounds for refusal are that disclosure is against national security interests; would break the law; involves information given in confidence by a third party; involves information relating specifically to an individual who has refused to allow it to be disclosed; would cause serious damage to the business; or involves information that is to be used to bring, prosecute or defend a legal action.

90. A trade union has submitted a claim to ACAS to be recognised as representing my employees for collective bargaining. I recognise no union at present and I do not intend to recognise this one.

Attempts at conciliation by ACAS will obviously be unsuccessful. They will then have to conduct an enquiry. Things will go in your favour if the inquiry reveals that combined actual and potential support for the trade union falls short of 50 per cent of the employees concerned (this will be established by ballot if necessary) or that the trade union does not have the necessary financial strength and experience.

91. ACAS has recommended that my company recognise a trade union. What can we now do to oppose this recommendation?

You may apply to ACAS for their recommendation to be revoked. If your application is rejected you then have two months before the trade union complains to ACAS. ACAS will again try to conciliate and if that fails the union may apply to the Central Arbitration Committee. If the CAC finds in favour of the union the terms and conditions that the CAC specifies will then become part of your employees' contracts of employment, enforceable through the courts.

92. I see a potential recognition claim looming. What should I do?

It depends on your outlook. You may wish to encourage the union for the benefit of future relations and to avoid industrial action. You may wish to take a neutral stance. Or you may attempt to cut the ground from under the union by giving good terms and conditions to employees and ensuring efficient communication between management and workers.

93. I own two companies. Because of industrial action by employees of one I have had to lay off employees of the other and they are claiming guarantee payments.

Employees are not entitled to guarantee payments where they are laid off because of a dispute involving other employees, or employees of an associated company.

94. I dismissed an employee giving him six weeks' notice. He then gave me a week's notice.

He is still treated as being dismissed by you, but if you require him to serve out the six weeks by serving another notice of this before his week's notice to you expires, his refusal may jeopardise his right to redundancy pay.

95. An employee swore at me in front of other employees so I sacked him. Now he is claiming unfair dismissal.

You may dismiss an employee fairly for misconduct only if it is of a serious nature. This particular case will have to be decided on its merits. It will be helpful if you can show that employees were aware that this would be considered a serious breach of discipline (see p. 120); that you had warned this employee about such incidents before; and that there had been other instances of misconduct by this employee.

96. I dismissed an employee for incompetence and naturally replaced him. He is now claiming unfair dismissal and demanding reinstatement. I am advised that he may succeed.
You will have to show that his incompetence was of a degree that justified dismissal having regard to all the circumstances, including past record etc. If the tribunal finds against you they will ignore the fact that you have employed a replacement unless you can show that the dismissed employee's work could only be done if a permanent replacement was found, or that you waited a reasonable time, were not informed by the dismissed employee that he wanted reinstatement or re-engagement, and only then engaged a permanent replacement because you could not reasonably cope otherwise. The tribunal will award compensation where re-engagement or reinstatement is not practicable.

97. I was forced to dismiss an employee unfairly because other employees refused to work with him.
A tribunal will make an award which will ignore the fact that the dismissal was forced upon you.

98. A tribunal has ordered re-engagement for unfair dismissal. I hate the man and have refused to have him on my premises.
The tribunal will make a basic award (the equivalent of redundancy pay); a compensatory award to cover the employee's financial loss resulting from the unfair dismissal and, unless you can show that since the tribunal made the re-engagement order changed circumstances have made it impracticable, an additional award for failure to re-engage. The additional award will be between thirteen and twenty-six weeks' pay except where dismissal was for trade union membership or activities, or was unlawful under the Race Relations or Sex Discrimination Acts, in which case the additional award will be between twenty-six and fifty-two weeks' pay.

99. I wish to dismiss an employee who is a shop steward.
Consultation with the union may avoid problems here.

100. A man applied for a job and I received from his then

employer a reference which spoke of the man in the most glowing terms. I now suspect that his previous employer was trying to get rid of him because the man has turned out to be totally incompetent and dishonest.

You may have a remedy against the man's previous employer for making a negligent statement.

101. A man telephoned me for a reference for an ex-employee and I was forced to tell him that the man was incompetent. The ex-employee has found out and is suing me for damages.

You may claim that the statement was justified, and that, in any event, it was made under qualified privilege as between one employer and another.

102. I have had to lay certain employees off for six of the last thirteen weeks. One of them has served notice on me that he intends to claim a redundancy payment; he would be entitled to the maximum £3,000.

If you wish to prevent this you must serve a counter-notice within seven days of receiving his, saying that you will contest liability because normal working will be resumed within four weeks and continue for at least thirteen. It will then be up to a tribunal to decide whether there is a reasonable prospect of normal working.

103. I took over a business four years ago but merely utilised the premises for a different trade. I retained some of the old employees and one of them who has been with me ever since is now, unfortunately, redundant. He is claiming redundancy pay for twenty years but he has only been with me for four.

Normally when a business changes hands service is considered to be continuous, so that an employee's entitlement to redundancy is calculated on the length of time he has worked for that business, irrespective of ownership. But in your case you did not purchase the business as a going concern and there has been a change of trade. Your employee should have made a redundancy claim against his old employer when you took over; he is now time-barred from doing that. He is entitled to only four years' redundancy pay from you.

104. B is not a union member so I did not consult with the union when I decided to make him redundant. They have now made a complaint.

If you recognise a trade union you must consult with them on redundancy whether the employee concerned is a member or not. You will now have to go through the whole procedure of conciliation through ACAS and a hearing before an industrial tribunal where that fails. The tribunal may make a protective award requiring you to pay the employee his normal money for up to twenty-eight days (if he is one of less than ten made redundant). But if you pay your employee any money under his contract of employment for any part of the protected period this money will be set against the award. In your defence you may argue that special circumstances made it impracticable for you to consult the union.

105. I have to make about a quarter of my work force redundant. Can I take this opportunity to weed out the poorest workers?

An employee may claim unfair dismissal if he considers that he has been unfairly selected for redundancy where other employees of his type have not been made redundant. You cannot make a selection on the grounds of trade union membership nor depart from a recognised procedure agreed for your company, such as last in, first out. If you do not recognise a union (and if ACAS has not recommended recognition), you have a freer hand and with cunning and skill may be able to achieve what you want.

106. I have to make some of my employees redundant. But I cannot afford the redundancy payments at present because of cash flow problems.

If you explain your problems to the Department of Employment, and can back up your claim with figures from your accountant, they will arrange for payment to your employees direct from the Redundancy Fund. You will then have to make repayment to the Fund when you are able. Do not merely refuse to make redundancy payments without consulting the Department as you may lose part of your entitlement to a rebate.

107. A sub-contractor working on the road through my com-

pany's housing development left a hole unlit at night. Someone fell into it and is now suing my company.

You are liable as you have a special duty to see that care is taken
where there might be danger to users of a highway. But you
have a claim against the sub-contractor.

**108. One of our commission agents has authority to accept
orders for up to £5,000 without referring to me. He was given
an order worth £10,000 which was ratified by the company on
10 March, but, meanwhile, the third party had withdrawn.**

The order would be binding as at the date it was taken (ratification would be retrospective) unless it was taken 'subject to
ratification'.

**109. Our selling agent has authority to bind the company on
orders up to £5,000 in value. He took an order worth £10,000,
which we cannot fulfil, and now the customer is suing for
breach of contract.**

The agent was undoubtedly acting within his apparent authority as far as the customer was concerned and the order would
therefore be binding unless the customer knew of the restriction
to the agent's authority.

**110. We have a dispute with an ex-agent who claims that we
owe him money. He has now gone to a retail customer of ours
and collected money that was due to us and kept it for himself
against the alleged debt.**

The retailer will still owe you the money if he knew you had terminated the agent's contract or if the agent had never been
authorised to collect money in the past. Otherwise your only
remedy is against the agent.

USEFUL BOOKS AND ADDRESSES

Atiyah, Patrick Selim, *Accidents, Compensation and the Law*
(Weidenfeld & Nicolson, 1976)
Borrie, Gordon J., *Commercial Law* (Butterworth, 1975)
Cooper, Sir William Mansfield, and John Crossley Wood (ed.),
Outlines of Industrial Law (Butterworth, 1972)
Hunt, Dennis D., *Employment and Dismissal Without Fear* (David
& Charles, 1979)

Schofield, P., and C. Burke, *Cases and Statutes on Labour Law* (Sweet & Maxwell, 1978)

Wallington, P., *Labour Statutes* (Butterworth, 1978)

Note: Labour law is a dynamic area and any book may need to be supplemented by the latest statutes.

Advisory, Conciliation and Arbitration Service
Head Office: Cleland House, Page Street, London SW1P 4ND
Department of Employment
8 St James's Square, London SW1
Trades Union Congress
Congress House, Great Russell Street, London WC1B 3LS

7
WINDING UP

In which we consider not only the rules of winding up but also what it is actually like to be put into compulsory liquidation.

One Man's Story

'When a bank forecloses it is really very simple. If you have previously been on bad terms you will receive a letter. If you have previously been on good terms you will also receive, in advance of the letter, a telephone call.

For me the call came on a Wednesday afternoon immediately after lunch. The man who telephoned was not the man I usually dealt with at the bank. He was not even his number two. He was the most junior person they could possibly have got to do it, unless they had asked a typist or one of the cleaners. He told me nicely, and had enough decency to sound hesitant and embarrassed, that the bank had decided to call in its loan, which was something over £700,000, and that I had until 12 o'clock the following Monday.

There were only two things for me to do. The first was to telephone the building site and have the men dismissed. The second was to telephone my accountant and inform him that for the main company involved in the site, a second company partly involved and a third property company that was bound to go down with the other two, the members had passed a winding-up resolution. One of my manufacturing companies stood to lose £20,000 but was in even worse trouble on the grounds that I would no longer be an acceptable guarantor for its borrowings.

On Monday the letter arrived one hour before the deadline of which it informed me. On Tuesday I heard that the bank had appointed a receiver for the building site and a security firm. On Wednesday loose materials on site began to disappear. As word got around, suppliers telephoned to find out what the

143

position was. Could they collect the materials that they had recently delivered? On Thursday I took the books of the three companies to my accountant.

A date was fixed for the creditors' meeting and notices were sent out. There were four weeks and I decided to take a holiday. When I returned my accountant told me that the bank had now put a value on the site and work-in-progress. They had lost half a million pounds.

THE MEETING OF CREDITORS

Any director fears the creditors' meeting if there is a deficiency. And he has particular reason to fear it if he has skimmed, manipulated figures, taken fraudulent preference or been negligent or incapable. I was afraid only on account of the deficiency. There were going to be a lot of angry men at the meeting and I was expecting abuse. On the other hand, I was myself the largest creditor after the main bank's half a million. My clearing bank and my manufacturing company at around £20,000 apiece were next. One supplier had lost £6,000, quite a few up to £5,000 and the sub-contractors anything up to £3,000 each, although there were many at just a few hundred. Of the sub-contractors, almost all had inflated what they were owed, no doubt expecting a dividend of some sort. Unfortunately, there was to be no dividend for unsecured creditors; the bank was realising its security and for the crumbs that were left the unsecured creditors ranked behind the costs and expenses of the winding-up, tax, rates, wages and salaries.

Let me give you some advice about choosing an accountant. He should be a man of imposing appearance and strong personality. I have attended creditors' meetings as a creditor and seen such a man as liquidator keep the meeting in order, keep tempers cool and keep issues in perspective. My accountant was not such a man. He let the creditors walk all over us. The meetings for the three companies, which were supposed to follow one after the other, somehow got jumbled up. It was a fiasco. The sub-contractors were bitter and the suppliers vicious. The worst of them all, the secretary of a public company, T—— Ltd, had sent a lorry to the site well after foreclosure to collect materials and had had it stopped by the police, which had made him mad.

Was my car owned by the company? Had the company ever received any writs? What was my track record in house-building? Had the company made me any loans? Why were there so few assets? Why and how had I borrowed so heavily on such a small capital base? Was the liquidator a friend of mine? Now they were getting nasty. The company secretary from T—— Ltd then called for a Department of Trade investigation. With plenty of public companies to be going on with, I doubt if the Department would have been interested; nevertheless two men nodded vigorously. My accountant was no help at all. When did I know about foreclosure? This man was not going to let up. Was it true that I was trading while insolvent?

The company secretary, who I later found out was called H——, then proposed "that this creditors' meeting does nothing but instead leaves it to me to present a petition for compulsory liquidation".

Motion proposed. Which company they were talking about I don't know, and neither did they. Motion carried. Only one man sitting in the front row dissented.

THE CREDITOR'S PETITION

The principal expression of any Mr Justice is one of benevolence. It is an expression that is suitable, with slight variation, for all occasions. "I could do worse," it says. "Be thankful that I am treating you so lightly." The only time that Mr Justice T—— lost this benevolent countenance was when the opposing counsel stated that I had bounced a cheque. News of this terrible deed reduced him to stuttering. It was the action of a bounder.

Had he enquired of me, or given me the chance to confer with my counsel, I would have been able to tell him that a cheque for £2,000 was stopped but that it was replaced by a cheque for £4,000.

Sometimes it is the little things, not the big issues, that shape your judgement of institutions, and that day my impression of British justice was not quite as it had been before.

Why couldn't I confer with counsel? I could not even get near him. Court no. 17 in the High Court of Justice in the Strand was packed with solicitors, clerks, petitioners, directors, shareholders, creditors, barristers; every seat was taken, people stood in the aisles and overflowed out into the corridor.

The number of cases in the Companies Court that year broke all previous records – 5,398 companies went into liquidation, nearly half compulsorily; one and a half thousand builders were bankrupted. The court dealt with compulsory windings-up at the rate of one a minute.

"Usual compulsory order."

"Usual compulsory order."

But not mine. The opportunity to observe Mr Justice T—— and the workings of the Companies Court was, of course, provided by my good friend H——, company secretary of T—— Ltd. For four weeks after the creditors' meetings I had heard nothing of any petition and began to believe I never would. My accountant was continuing with his duties as liquidator because the creditors had not voted for his removal and therefore his appointment by the members, that is the shareholders, that is, basically me, still held good. Then the petition was forwarded from my old offices. Obviously H—— was aiming to make me responsible for company debts over the trading while insolvent allegation, hoping the Official Receiver would be able to prove what my accountant might ignore. Unfortunately H—— had made a simple mistake. Those old offices were no longer the registered office of the company, and on those grounds I decided to oppose the petition.

The case was adjourned for fourteen days to give me the proper time to consider the petition. I had been expecting it to be dismissed in accordance with my thick company law book, but I soon learned that the court is always on the side of the petitioner. I understand that sympathy; I did not like being on the wrong end of it.

When I saw my accountant I discovered that H—— had made yet another mistake. Three companies were in liquidation but H—— had gone for the compulsory liquidation of only one of them. Presumably he thought the activities of that particular company the most suspicious. Unfortunately for him that particular company did not happen to owe him any money, and if you are not owed you cannot petition.

At the second court hearing my counsel stated, with the backing of the liquidator, that no money was owed to the petitioner. The petitioners asked for time to consider our submission and were given an adjournment for fourteen days.

At the third court hearing the petitioners agreed that no goods had ever been delivered to the company, but their counsel said that he had had it brought to his notice that although another of my companies had actually been invoiced for the goods, a cheque had nevertheless been received from the petitioned company and the cheque had bounced. He requested time to take fuller instructions – adjournment for fourteen days. (That was the day, you will recall, that Mr Justice T——'s benevolent smile slipped.)

At the fourth court hearing, the counsel for the petitioners was still without detailed instructions. My counsel was not. He began his major speech. But a major speech, apparently, was not allowed. It was too time-consuming. The case was adjourned until that afternoon. That afternoon expensive counsel and I sat through another twenty boring cases, but ours was not called. It was adjourned until the next day.

At the fifth court hearing my counsel was finally able to present the very simple facts that the petitioners were not owed any money. Case adjourned; only this time, since it was the end of term, the adjournment would have to be for ten weeks until the start of the next term. According to my counsel this was not at all unusual. One man he knew of in a case similar to mine had managed to keep things going for over a year.

Solicitors are always urging you to settle out of court and now I see why. So we did settle out of court. H—— withdrew the petition and paid me £100 to cover my costs. (It didn't cover them.) End of round one.

Round two: a new petition was correctly served against the right company.

According to my company law book I could oppose on the grounds that the money claimed was not owed. I had had enough trouble with that one when it was true. A second defence might be that the other creditors were in favour of the voluntary liquidation continuing – not true. A third was what the book called "improper motive". I could allege that H—— was trying to cover up his attempted theft of materials from the site by having my accountant removed, but this was too fantastic.

I bowed to the inevitable, ignored the subsequent hearing and eventually received the following two notices from the Official Receiver:

TAKE NOTICE that a Winding-up Order in the matter of the above-named Company was made on the . . . day of . . . and I have in pursuance of the provisions of the Companies Act, 1948, and Companies (Winding-up) Rules 1949, TO REQUIRE you to submit to me, within fourteen days of the date of the said Winding-up Order, a Statement of Affairs, in duplicate, of the said Company.

With reference to the winding-up order made against the above-named company, I have to ask you to attend at this office on Thursday next, the . . . at 10.30am for the purpose of giving information as to the company's assets and affairs. Please ask for Room No . . . at Atlantic House as above.

Please bring with you, or arrange to forward to this office forthwith, a list, with addresses, of the creditors of the company, and all books, papers, documents, etc., relating to the company's affairs which are in your possession or under your control.

THE OFFICIAL RECEIVER

Atlantic House is on Holborn Viaduct, close to where it goes over Farringdon Street. A porter unloaded the six cardboard boxes full of books and papers from the boot of my car in pouring rain.

L—— met me in reception and conducted me to his office, which was like a schoolroom with painted two-tone walls, bare except for an 'In Case of Fire' notice. There were two cheap desks, two tall grey metal cabinets, two filing cabinets, a view towards the Barbican and the green roof of Smithfield Market. And the six cardboard boxes.

To feel him out I said, "You must be busy the way things are at the moment."

"Your company is the 2,490th in compulsory liquidation so far this year. In a normal year there are about 400 cases."

He handed me a typed notice sellotaped to cardboard. The Perjury Act 1911, Section 5(c). I must not lie.

L—— switched on a tape recorder on his desk and dictated into it my answers to questions that he read from a printed booklet.

"What is your full name . . . Have you ever used any other name . . . What is the registered office . . . What is the share capital . . . How were you financed . . . What assets exist . . . Where are they . . .?" And so on. Only at the end was I asked when the company became insolvent.

"The company was never insolvent until the bank foreclosed. We went into voluntary liquidation immediately. Unless you define insolvency in a different way to me."

148

"Insolvency is the inability to meet bills as they fall due."

"Then I stick with that answer."

"To what do you attribute the failure of the company?"

"To the bank foreclosing."

"That is not a proper explanation. You must say something more than that."

"To high interest rates and the stagnation of the housing market."

The session had taken two hours.

"Wouldn't it have been easier to send me the questions? Then I could have prepared full answers."

"We don't want you to have time to think up answers. You will have to come back for a further interview in about a week, once all this has been typed up. It will be a bit more searching than this one."

L—— gave me a look which seemed to say: "We know you're on the fiddle. Everybody is on the fiddle. What we're going to do about it depends on how I feel."

"How do you manage to wade through all that paper?" I asked, perhaps too obviously.

"We don't."

He handed me a thick pile of forms.

"Get your accountant to fill these in. It's the statement of affairs. I'll see you next week. We get some pretty unsavoury characters in here," he said finally and for no reason.

I hoped he meant that I was not one.

My second interview came only a few days after clearing bank base rate hit 15 per cent.

"Busy?" I asked.

"I have had to deal with forty building firms in compulsory liquidation during the past week," said L——.

On this occasion I was to be grilled by his boss, P——. P—— handed me my statement from the previous meeting, headed:

IN RE:

No. 002490 of . . .

Statement made by . . ., director, at Atlantic House, Holborn Viaduct, E.C.I.

'My attention has been drawn to Section 5(c) of the Perjury Act 1911. I understand that Section and its implications and the following is my statement to the best of my knowledge, information and belief . . .'

"Do you wish to add to or amend your statement?"

I made some corrections and signed it. P—— then produced a bound book rather like a company minute book. He asked me the 133 standard questions in it and wrote my answers beside them in longhand. There was no tape-recorder.

"Did you ever mortgage any shares . . . Did you sell shares . . . Did you sell land to associated companies . . . Has any employee contributed to the downfall of the company . . .?" And on and on.

I knew from his comments that P—— had not been through the books, at least, not in any detail. He asked me no questions connected with any entries in them. In fact, I had already calculated that the maximum time that could be spent on an average company would be forty man hours. Not much.

Not enough for the Official Receiver to catch anybody out, unless he happened to have done something obvious like drawing a big cash sum the day before everything collapsed.

"What happens next?"

"There will be a creditors' meeting in about two months' time. I will not need to see you again beforehand. After the creditors' meeting then as far as I am concerned everything for you will be over."

THE STATEMENT OF AFFAIRS

A recorded delivery letter arrived from the Official Receiver:

I refer to the notice sent to you on . . . requiring you to submit a statement of affairs and supporting documents in this matter.

I would remind you that the statement of affairs supported by accounts covering the period . . . to . . . has not yet been submitted to me and I shall be grateful if you will let me know within the next seven days what steps are being taken in connection with its preparation.

A month had gone by since I sent the printed forms to my accountant, so I telephoned and he said he would get on with them.

About ten days later I received another recorded delivery from the Official Receiver. The packet contained Form C.73 (Rule 125) giving the date of the 'first' meetings of creditors and contributories and requiring my presence as managing director; form C.71 (Rule 122) inviting my presence at the creditors' meeting in my capacity as a creditor; a blue proxy form; pink and green voting papers; and an affidavit to be sworn. On the latter I entered that I was owed £75,000. It was somewhat on the high side but I wanted to be sure that I would have plenty of voting power at the meeting. I took the affidavit to a commissioner for oaths.

"Don't tell me about it," he said. "Only yesterday one of my biggest clients went into liquidation."

P——telephoned.

"We have not received the statement of affairs or accounts."

"But you've already called the creditors' meeting. I assumed my accountant had done them."

"No, I have heard nothing from him at all. He hasn't even accounted to me for the monies that he has."

"I can't understand it. I definitely instructed him. Don't you need the statement of affairs at the creditors' meeting?"

"It is helpful. But not essential."

H——of T—— Ltd would love that. No statement of affairs. He'd really go to town on me.

"I will have to get a court order", P—— continued, "unless I get this statement of affairs soon. And then if you do not comply you will be in contempt of court."

I telephoned my accountant.

"What accounts?" he said. "You never instructed me to prepare any accounts."

"But I gave you all those forms from the Official Receiver."

There was a long pause. I could hear his brain working. I knew what he was thinking. ("Oh, *those* papers. I suppose I should have looked at them. But he is virtually bankrupt. Probably can't pay me for what I've done already.")

"I can't use the funds I'm holding," he said at last. He had a few hundred pounds from the sale of some uncharged assets.

"How much will it cost?"

"Three hundred pounds."

I phoned back to P——.

"This is going to cost £400. I can't afford that kind of money. Let the petitioners pay. They wanted this."

"It is the directors' responsibility. Either you can use an accountant or you can do it yourself."

"You mean I can prepare the accounts myself?"

"Of course. I cannot let you have the books back, but you can come here and I will give you the facilities."

To think what I could have got away with. So this was what H—— had been fighting for. He thought the Official Receiver would give me a rough time. If only he knew.

E—— chaired the "first" creditors' meeting, boss of P——, and L——. He read a history of the company prepared from my statement. He said there would be no money available for the ordinary creditors. He said there was no statement of affairs ready.

Nobody objected. No one said anything much, except inevitably H—— who made a speech about why he wanted a compulsory liquidation.

E—— said he imagined the meeting would want to confirm the Official Receiver as liquidator, there being no funds.

I waited for H—— to propose his own accountants but he said nothing.

E—— asked me whether I was in agreement. How funny if I had proposed my own accountant and used my £75,000 voting power to try to force it through. But I said nothing either.

In the end it had all been for just one thing. H—— needed to report to the board of T—— Ltd that he had done everything possible to recover money from my company. In fact he had done nothing except waste his own time and throw more money away. But the board wouldn't know that.

THE PERSONAL GUARANTEES

I refer to your letter of . . . and our subsequent telephone conversations on Friday last concerning the offer you would like to make in settlement of your guarantee on behalf of . . . Ltd.

I have to advise you that such an offer against a debt of this magnitude requires the consideration and directives of the Credit Committee and you are, of course, aware that they have received detailed progress reports on the development over many months.

You will be contacted again as soon as possible after the next Committee Meeting.

I was. The offer referred to was refused. A meeting was

arranged with the ominously titled Collections Manager.

"Age?"

"My age?"

"Yes. I have to assess your earning potential over the rest of your working life."

Then there was the letter from my clearing bank's solicitor.

My clients . . . have consulted me in connection with your liability to them under a Guarantee dated . . . relating to the above account . . .

I am instructed to give you a final seven days from today's date in which to let me have your remittance in settlement of your liability to my Clients, failing which my Clients have my advice to institute proceedings against you without further notice.

On that one I was lucky. The guarantee was for only half the deficiency.

Then there was the letter regarding the manufacturing company.

With reference to the Guarantee dated . . . for £ . . . given by you for the above account, we regret it has now become necessary to call upon you for the payment of the sum of £ . . .

That I had expected. The manufacturing company would have to go down with the rest.

It may take me eleven years to write the end of this story because, under the Limitation Acts, a man may not be sued for breach of a deed after the elapse of twelve years, and one has now gone by.

But I think I will do a deal with that Collections Manager. He is like the sheriff who has been told to bring the outlaw in alive. Get this man, the Credit Committee said, and bring him in solvent. Bankrupt he's no good to us. Solvent at least he's got income. And we know it isn't nice to make a man bankrupt.'

PROBLEMS AND SOLUTIONS

111. I wish to wind up my company which is solvent.

It is a simple matter to dissolve a company that has ceased trading and has neither assets nor liabilities, simply by informing the Registrar of Companies. Presumably your company is not in this category. Members of the company may vote for a voluntary winding-up and appoint a liquidator and if a majority of the directors have previously made a declaration of solvency – that is, stated that the company will be able to meet all its liabilities within twelve months – the members remain in control of the winding-up. But if the company later proves unable to meet its debts it becomes a creditors' voluntary winding-up. The creditors may appoint a different liquidator and the directors may face criminal charges over their declaration of solvency.

112. I am being accused of trading while insolvent.

If a company continues to incur debts when there is no prospect of the creditors being paid, then the court may infer that the company was being carried on with intent to defraud and knowing parties may be made personally liable for the debts. Your defence must be either that the company was not insolvent during the period referred to or that you were not aware that it was insolvent.

A company is insolvent either when it is unable to meet its debts as they fall due for payment or if its assets are not sufficient to meet its liabilities. But a company that proves to be insolvent under the last definition on a winding-up may not have been insolvent while it was trading; a winding-up generally diminishes the value of assets.

113. I wish to wind up my company which is insolvent.

The members must pass a winding-up resolution in general meeting and since the directors will have been unable to make a declaration of solvency it will be a creditors' voluntary winding-up. A members' meeting must then be called and a creditors' meeting to follow it by not more than twenty-four hours. Failure to call a creditors' meeting would be extremely suspicious and the creditors will in any case be entitled to apply to the court to have one called. A statement of affairs and list of creditors must be laid before the creditors' meeting, which is presided over by one of the directors. The creditors may appoint a liquidator, in which case the liquidator chosen by the members in their meeting will not be appointed, or the creditors may accept the members' choice. The creditors may also appoint a committee of inspection and the creditors and the members may each appoint up to five persons to represent them on it. The liquidator will investigate any obvious irregularities and any less obvious that are brought to his attention; he will dispose of assets, pay himself out of the proceeds and apply the balance to meeting the claims of creditors as far as possible. The company will then be dissolved, the entire process taking probably one to two years.

114. A creditor is making threatening noises about having the company compulsorily wound up.

Your creditor presumably intends to petition to have the company wound up on the grounds that it is unable to pay its debts and must therefore establish this in one of the following ways:

1. By serving on the company at its registered office a signed demand for payment for a debt of £200 or more. If you do not settle within three weeks the petition may proceed and your only defence then will be show that the money is not owed in which case the winding-up order will be refused.

2. If a judgement creditor, by showing that a process of execution has not been satisfied.

3. By showing that the company's assets are not sufficient to meet its liabilities or that it cannot meet its debts as they fall due for payment or that the directors have admitted insolvency etc. A creditor is unlikely to be able to demonstrate insolvency satisfactorily under this category.

115. A creditor has alleged and asked the liquidator to investigate fraudulent preference.

If within six months before the commencement of a winding-up a company that is insolvent pays money or transfers or charges property to a creditor giving him preference over others, then it may be considered fraudulent. A classic example would be where a company pays off an overdraft guaranteed by the directors so as to relieve them. A fraudulent preference is void. To refute the allegations you should demonstrate one of the following facts:

1. The company was solvent at the time the benefit was given.

2. The benefit was not given voluntarily – legal proceedings were threatened.

3. There was no intention to give an improper advantage to the creditor.

4. The creditor received no benefit that he would not have got anyway if the company had been wound up at the time.

USEFUL BOOKS

Collins, Hugh (ed.), *Bankruptcy in County Courts* (7th ed., Oyez, 1978)

Redmond, P. W. D., *Bankruptcy Law* (Macdonald & Evans, 1973)

Thompson, J. H. (ed.), *Sale's Law Relating to Bankruptcy, Liquidations and Receiverships* (Macdonald & Evans, 1977)

INDEX